Pragmatic Data Management

Using the DMBOK to build and sustain your data management capability

Andy Peyton
for DAMA Australia

Kindle version ISBN:	978-1-7647181-0-3
eBook version ISBN:	978-1-7647181-1-0
Print version ISBN:	978-1-7647181-2-7

Cover designed by Getcovers.

CONTENTS

PREFACE

The hidden problem

There's a huge problem in most organisations that most people aren't aware of, and it's quietly growing like cancer. Data managers have seen it developing, but while it's been manageable until now, it may be getting to the point where it's out of control and it could spell disaster for some organisations. That problem is the assumption that proper data management is being performed.

Why is this important?

In the past, most data was held in operational systems and it was these systems that captured, organized, and reported on data. If there was a problem with the data, users of the system tended to recognise it and get it fixed – usually because it directly impacted their customer service. Data fields in the database often mapped directly to fields on their screens.

Over time, we started to move our data into data warehouses, and we started using this data for our corporate reporting and business intelligence. However, the people who exploited this warehouse data were different to the people who relied on the data day-to-day, and they could be unaware of data anomalies that the operational users experienced – to these data analysts, the warehouse data was, by default, assumed to be fit-for-purpose.

More recently we started replicating key data into other data stores, like search systems, operational data stores, data lakes, data caches, etc. In modern systems it's not uncommon to have core operational data replicated to multiple stores across the IT system landscape.

Data specialists are aware that the migration of data to these data stores often involves assumptions about the data and that sometimes misunderstanding occurs. The meaning of source fields is sometimes assumed, the data gets transformed into something else during the transfer, data is merged with other data, or simply the data is misunderstood. As a result, the downstream consumers of the data can be unaware that the information they are relying on may be being poisoned by multiple data problems.

Data management in many organisations is set up to support operational systems and databases only and its authority is rarely extended to cover the broader management of the organisation's data. We often do not see the same formal data management processes existing for databases and data stores that hold data that has been propagated from the source operational systems. The drive for reporting agility can result in a focus on rapid development and deployment rather than robust design documentation. There is likely to be no-one actively working to monitor and improve data quality and integrity across all consumers of data - data tends to be passed from silo to silo, with each team only considering its own silo.

Today, we are heading at break-neck speed into the world of AI and again the assumption is made that the data used to teach these AI engines is accurate and correctly understood. Professional data managers see the risk of compounding data errors that result in incorrect advice. A foundation of data quality problems, transformation errors, and misunderstanding data can lead to the progressive poisoning of the data that AI engines rely on.

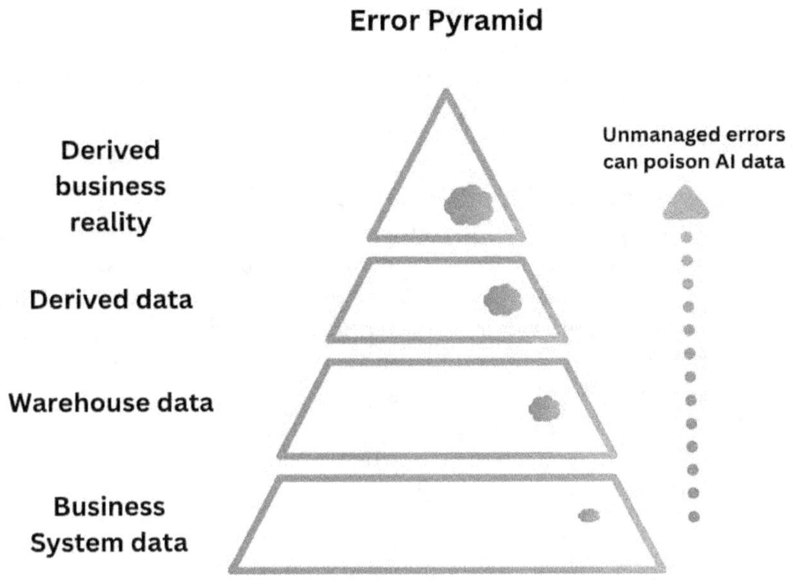

I've got a real example.

> I was once a data administrator for a government agency that distributed money to many citizens. There was a bug in an operational system that incorrectly issued over-payments for customers under certain situations. In these cases, the business system users wrote off the debt, but over time payments got larger and users didn't have permission to write off the larger debt amounts. However, they found they could write off the debt with two or more partial write-off transactions. Operationally, we all knew what was happening and the system still delivered the right service, so the bug never got a high priority, and the practice was allowed to continue.
>
> Later, it was noted that a draft business intelligence report had observed an increase in the number of write-off transactions, and assumed (incorrectly) that an increasing number of customers were having debt written off.
>
> Following on from this, a subsequent policy analysis suggested that the national economy was getting worse because the number of debt write-offs per capita was increasing.

> There was a very uncomfortable meeting with lots of finger-pointing when we got everybody in the room and worked the problem through. It became clear that a form of "Chinese whispers" was taking place with the errors compounding as information became progressively derived from the underlying data. Unfortunately, it is difficult to record this type of business practice in traditional metadata.

What would happen if an AI engine had access to the underlying data? It would surely have no knowledge of the underlying operational reality of the data and its meaning. There can be a significant amount of business knowledge that isn't captured in the underlying data. Would an AI engine that only looks at the enterprise data just infer that the economy was getting worse? Would a person getting that inference from the AI engine have any idea that the answer they got was wrong?

In the end, it was a data management process that saved the day. Fortunately, the organisation in question at the time had the best data management practice that I've ever seen.

Unfortunately, that level of data management practice is now quite rare.

The suicidal risk of doing nothing

While AI currently has a lot of focus because of its potential for misleading its consumers when relying on poor quality data, organisations may be risking suicide if they do nothing about data management.

We are aware that system architectures are continuing to evolve at an ever-increasing rate, with data being stockpiled in multiple locations including cloud databases and SaaS solutions. Graduate IT staff rarely arrive with any training in data management, and we generally rely on more experienced staff providing them with guidance and wisdom. However, as our data landscape becomes more complex and experienced staff retire, we'll need the support of ingrained processes to ensure that data disasters are averted. Organisations that don't have data management processes in place run the severe risk of having their critical data managed by people who have inherited a data-oriented job, have no formal qualification in managing data, and are likely unaware of the critical consequences of data loss or corruption. I've experienced situations where nobody knew what data backups were being taken and Production scripts had to be investigated to see what was actually being done.

Data management professionals recognise the risks to the quality of organisation's information when good data management practice is missing. This can result in:

- data being misunderstood and misinterpreted
- data quality problems poisoning derived data
- the inability to reuse data for other purposes or link it with other data
- data not being adequately secured from theft or accidental loss
- personal data being accidentally leaked publicly.

Consider the consequences of doing nothing in a reality where we are collecting an increasingly large amount of data, distributing our data across multiple systems as well as SaaS systems outside our control, while trying to manage our data with inexperienced IT workers trying to do their best as individuals without a team and a system to back them up.

A call to action

For reasons I explain later in this book, data management suffers from being a "hidden" service provided by IT departments. Most executives in an organisation likely assume that good data management is happening automatically, and they have no reason to question this assumption. In a way, this is correct if the operational systems appear to be collecting and displaying their data correctly. However, they fail to understand all the data interpretation that takes place after being recorded in the operational databases and the institutional knowledge that is not being captured in data derivations and analyses.

At its core, data management is a risk mitigation strategy. It addresses multiple risks, including:

- not knowing what your data means
- misinterpreting your data
- corrupting or losing all your data
- not knowing what data you have and why you have it
- what the data can and can't be used for

- making sure you're meeting your regulatory requirements for handling data, such as leaking personal data

In an AI-enabled environment, it can also help mitigate the risk of bad business decision making and giving bad advice to customers.

Because it is a hidden IT service, data management is generally under-funded and sometimes non-existent. This is not because of deliberate action, but usually because people don't know what formal data management involves and the risks it was set up to mitigate.

This book seeks to help you create a successful data management practice and embed it within the organisation where it is valued and supported. Achieving this requires an understanding of basic management theory as well as a knowledge of your own organisation's business drivers.

INTRODUCTION

This book is designed for anyone who wants to build a formal data management capability within an organisation or would like to extend the existing capability. It will also be useful to someone that wants to ensure that their existing data management capabilities are recognised by senior management for the value that it delivers to the organisation.

The DAMA Data Management Book of Knowledge[1] is a document that will be referred to regularly. This document is a great starting point for data management techniques and practices, but it won't help you with the business process of establishing and maintaining good data management. *Pragmatic Data Management* will assist with filling this gap, because difficulty in establishing and sustaining data management in an organisation has little to do with technology or process and more to do with your organisation's management, internal politics, and experience with data.

Data management is one of the least understood generalist areas of IT. I say generalist because it involves a set of practices and processes that are common across all technologies, as opposed to specialist areas such as AI machine learning. Many IT professionals will have no knowledge of AI technologies, but with data management, we are talking about governance processes, standards, backups, and a range of other areas that most IT folks are quite familiar with.

---

[1] DAMA-DMBOK: Data Management Body of Knowledge (2nd Edition), July 2017

While an IT professional may be quite comfortable discussing data backups specifically, they are often unfamiliar with the concept of backups needing to be defined and managed in accordance with a broader data management responsibility across all the organisation's datasets. I've rarely seen any data administrator link a particular system backup strategy to an enterprise data threat assessment.

If you break data management down into individual components and discuss it with other IT professionals, then they'll always agree that each component is important for the organisation overall and the IT department specifically. But look around, and you'll rarely ever see a dedicated Data Management team tasked with managing all these processes in an integrated, coordinated, and professional way.

When we discuss data with senior management, we usually hear some or all the following beliefs expressed:

- Data is vitally important to the organisation.
- We want our data protected.
- We want to do more with our data.
- We want more of our people to use data analytics when making decisions.
- We expect that in the future we'll be powering our organisation with AI coupled with our extensive repository of data.
- We haven't heard about any data problems

When you ask the Executive team who has responsibility for the organisation's data, fingers usually point at the Chief Information Officer (CIO) and the IT department generally, with an assumption that they are managing it all. However, you will rarely see any form of formal reporting back to the Executive about the management and security of the enterprise data. Once again, there is an assumption that the data is being adequately managed by the IT department. Most importantly, there is often very little recognition that the Executive themselves have a role in an enterprise's data management – by setting high-level requirements for the organisation's data management landscape.

Pragmatic Data Management has been developed to either kick-start your internal data management practice, or to ensure that an existing data management team remains visible, relevant, and most importantly – funded.

What's different about this book?

There are many books that talk about the theory of data management or various data management techniques and skills. However, they often fail to address some key threats to growing and sustaining your data management practice:

- a lack of engagement with, and support from, the Executive team
- most people in the organisation, including IT professionals, don't know what is meant by the term "data management"
- data management must compete for funds and resources against other IT teams
- data management isn't seen as delivering customer services and can be seen as overhead
- IT infrastructural improvements are delivered via projects, so data management improvements don't get funded or resourced unless a project requires them
- data management is seen as an internal IT function that is assumed to be operating effectively – it is not normally a "squeaky wheel" within the organisation.

Pragmatic Data Management is focused on techniques for combatting some of the pressures that will impede the establishment and enhancement of your data management practice. It is based on many years' experience in data management across many organisations including both the public and private sectors – from small, nimble companies to major government departments.

Data Management Book of Knowledge

This document should be read in conjunction with the DAMA International Data Management Book of Knowledge (aka DMBOK). The DMBOK provides data management professionals with an internationally-recognised standard for data management standards and processes that can be usefully leveraged to gain both professional recognition of data management, and acceptance of data management as a cohesive set of data-related functions that need to be managed for the benefit of an organisation.

However, the DMBOK is not a guide to the implementation of a sustainable data management practice.

It does have "thunk factor". That is, it makes a nice "thunk" sound when you drop it on someone's desk, so they recognise that maybe there's more to data management than they think.

You should be aware that not everyone will have any concept of what is meant by a "body of knowledge", so it will be useful for you to inform yourself about other BOKs that exist and the disciplines that use them. Examples of other internationally-recognised BOKs include:

- IMBOK (information management)
- EABOK (enterprise architecture)
- BABOK (business analysis)
- PMBOK (project management)
- HRBOK (human resources)

Pragmatic data management

The philosophy behind this book is that good data management doesn't mean that you must implement everything in the DMBOK. It means that you've implemented what your business needs at a given point in time.

While it can be important to implement the industry standard practices described in DMBOK, building a successful data management practice requires that you focus initially on the urgent and important data management activities and from there continue to extend your capabilities. Robotically implementing data management practices without considering what your business really needs is more likely to result in failure and ultimately de-funding of data management because you may have spent valuable time and effort delivering things that no-one considers valuable.

While this book focuses on the establishment of a successful and self-sustaining data management practice, hopefully subsequent books will address how to pragmatically implement more specific practices such as:

- identifying threats to your data and how to protect against them
- implementing data quality monitoring so that you know where your data problems are and what they are costing your organisation
- managing data problems that can grow in your data warehouse and compromise the intelligence that you gain from it, especially if you are using it for AI learning
- assembling a data architecture for your organisation that delivers benefits and isn't just a large set of pretty diagrams that can fall into disuse because they don't actually help the data development, data consumption, or system building process.

The structure of this book

This book is laid out in an order that should help in the establishment of data management capabilities within an organisation. The objective of each chapter is described below.

- *Challenges to be Overcome* addresses the business environment that IT, and data management in particular, exists within, and the organisational issues that will likely resist the implementation of formal data management. It identifies blockers that need to be overcome and provides suggestions on how to do this.
- *Planning Your Data Management Journey* discusses how to plan the establishment of formal data management from the perspectives of developing a formal strategy, as well as developing an internal plan for gaining recognition of the need for establishing a data management team.

- *Starting Formal Data Management* provides guidance on where to start formal data management and some ideas for engaging with executives and senior data stakeholders.
- *Collecting Data Management Requirements* provides ideas for beginning the process of understanding your organisation's current data problems and how to use this to introduce stakeholders to the concepts of the Data Management Body of Knowledge (DMBOK).
- *Developing a Data Management Strategy* outlines an approach to developing a formal Data Management Strategy that builds upon the previously completed work and the established relationships.
- *Being Pragmatic About Your Development Artifacts* discusses how to be pragmatic about the artifacts that you will be delivering, and to avoid producing documents that end up as shelfware – never to be used. Being pragmatic means producing work that is "good enough" for the subsequent work.
- *Being Pragmatic In How You Work* discusses how to be pragmatic about deciding which activities you'll progress initially and those that you'll defer. It's important to understand the current business need to deliver benefits early, and the need for quick wins to solidify support.
- *Bringing It All Together* discusses how to bring all this guidance together to establish a data management capability that is valued within the organisation and hopefully resistant to budget cuts.

CHALLENGES TO BE OVERCOME

Before you can build an effective data management capability you need to understand the modern IT business environment and the roadblocks that this environment will be putting in your way.

You need to recognise the specific blockers in your path if you are going to defeat them. And you must defeat or at least nullify them if you want to be successful. No-one wins a race by deliberately running with a blindfold.

Why you need to defeat the blockers

There is sound theory behind the need to defeat blockers, notably Herzberg's Two-Factor Theory. Herzberg suggested that motivation and demotivation are separate factors and not two sides of the same coin. You cannot successfully motivate someone if they are simultaneously being demotivated. In order to motivate, you first need to remove or reduce the demotivating factors.

Consider your own workplace – you may recognise one or more of the following demotivating or motivating factors.

Factors that demotivate people include:

- a toxic culture where your co-workers don't care about doing a good job
- poor office equipment and atmosphere
- unrealistic deadlines
- inability to see the value in your contribution
- feeling underpaid
- being expected to work extra hours without additional pay

- being expected to respond to emails and text messages out of working hours
- changes in direction that mean your previous efforts have been thrown away

Factors that motivate people include:

- receiving recognition and respect from peers and management
- feeling part of a team that works well together and fun to work with
- job security and achievable career progression
- understanding how your work contributes to business success
- appreciating how your organisation's work helps the broader community
- seeing a demonstrable success

Are you going to be motivated to do your best if you hate coming into work every day, or you see incompetent people receiving promotions? Would you be more motivated if you worked with a great team of professionals who recognised your contributions and gave you the support you need?

Consider how this theory applies to building your data management capability:

- Can you get funding if senior management doesn't understand its relevance?
- Can you get IT resources if the CIO doesn't understand what you actually do?
- Will you get support from your IT peers if they don't know what you mean by "data management"?
- Can you get support for introducing data governance controls if people don't understand the risks they are ignoring?

We need to identify the specific demotivating blockers so that a mitigation strategy can be implemented for each of them. Ideally there won't be too many!

Of course, not all organisations have the same blockers. You might have some that are unique, but there could be others that you share with many other organisations. There may be some comfort in realising that you are not alone in dealing with these blockers and that many others in your position in other organisations are also dealing with the same problems.

An additional benefit of reviewing common blockers is that it may prompt you to consider your unique challenges and possible ways to overcome them.

Common blockers to good data management

In the following sections, we'll look at some common blockers and how to address them. These include:

- the modern, no-frills methodology where IT departments are expected to do more with less budget and resources
- management's lack of understanding of what data management is, its potential scope, and the business value that it brings
- management's lack of understanding of the risks to their data that can be mitigated by good data management
- business believing that data is a problem to be managed by the IT department without acknowledging their ownership of the data
- data managers needing to compete with application development teams for funding and resources
- the data management deficiency seeming insurmountable
- vendors engaging with senior management and promising that their data management tools are a silver bullet that will solve the organisation's problems

Let's examine each of these in the following sections.

The modern no-frills IT methodology

Today, all organisations seek to minimize their operational expenses. Reduced expenses mean more profit (or perhaps bigger executive bonus payments!).

Traditionally, IT has been a significant expense and in the current economic climate, management is always seeking to do more with less. This dramatically impacts how IT investments are viewed.

Current IT drivers impacting data management include:

- time-to-market – management dislikes anything that appears to slow down implementing a product
- data management functionality may not be seen as important as application functionality
- IT solutions are developed via projects, so without a project sponsor it can be difficult to get new initiatives off the ground. Business sponsors often don't actively support "internal" IT improvements.
- great new ideas from senior management that must be prioritised

For many commercial organisations, *time-to-market* is a key driver. Management wants to get their product into the marketplace as soon as possible, and as a result, anything that slows this is seen as a problem. If data management requirements are seen as slowing the development process, then complaints and resistance can be expected. Similarly, in government, politicians often want to announce a new policy initiative and then deliver it as soon as possible so that they are still around to claim credit for it.

In the eyes of business users, *application functionality* is paramount. Application functionality is usually all that is visible to customers, so success is gauged by application features – a whole world of complexity can be represented by a button on the screen that results in wonderful things. By comparison, data management functionality is usually in the background; even though it provides important benefits to the organisation, it can be difficult to justify to business system owners. If developing a proposed new data management feature has to compete against additional application functionality, the application enhancement will most likely win because the business owners can more directly see how their users will benefit – they may not care that a back-end backup process is inefficient because it doesn't directly impact them.

The typical IT department delivers new applications and services via a series of *projects*. Many organisations have project management offices (PMOs), project portfolio management, or some other enterprise solution for allocating funds to projects, setting milestones and deliverables, monitoring and reporting progress, and controlling scope. It can be difficult, or even impossible, to get approval for enterprise solutions, especially those related to data management, unless they can be piggybacked off a business-oriented project. The massive overspending on IT around the time of the dot-com boom-and-bust resulted in many IT departments having their investment budgets transferred to business teams to ensure that IT was only delivering what the business wanted and not chasing new IT toys. The downside is that funds for back-end system improvements, including data management initiatives, also have to be allocated from the business. IT often only has a budget for established business-as-usual operations, so unless something can be funded by internal savings, getting funding for new data management initiatives can be challenging.

The four-dollar problem

A data management problem that I've encountered regularly is what I call "the four-dollar problem". In this scenario, when supporting a new initiative, we encounter a recurring enterprise weakness that we think should be fixed once-and-for-all. Overcoming this problem costs time and money, but we'd like to fix it and avoid having to repeatedly re-solve it for future projects. Let's say that developing a comprehensive enterprise solution will cost $4 – however when we present this idea to the project manager, they invariably ask for the project-specific cost. When you say it will only cost $3, they tell you to go with that – because they are not tasked with solving enterprise solutions, only their specific project ones. Project managers are usually conditioned to minimise their project scope and costs and are unwilling to deliver broad enterprise solutions.

Over time, we end up spending $20 on multiple point-solutions when a single $4 fix would have sufficed. Furthermore, after spending our $20 we still lack an enterprise solution and instead have five different solutions for the same problem.

The great new idea problem

The modern IT landscape also suffers from the "great new idea" problem, where a senior manager conceives of, or supports, a new initiative that wasn't in any prior development strategy or schedule. The IT department gets directed to support this initiative using existing resources. This results in IT management looking for IT activities that can be downsized or paused without visibly damaging or delaying more visible business-oriented projects - data management activities may unwillingly become targets.

Management knows nothing about data management

After many decades, it's clear that data management hasn't embedded itself in the consciousness of IT management as a distinct discipline. What we see as components of data management are often seen as just a group of data-related tasks scattered across the IT operations landscape. Within some large organisations, previously dedicated data management teams have been disbanded and the work distributed to other teams. In the commercial sector, you're either seen as revenue-generating or an overhead, and data management is usually seen as the latter. We have to deal with the likelihood that IT management and technical teams have had no experience treating data management as a cohesive discipline.

Within this likely IT environment, data management enthusiasts often have to deal with the following problems:

- The CIO doesn't understand what we mean by data management and its possible scope and complexity.
- The CIO assumes that good data management is already taking place because they haven't heard any complaints.
- The organisation's executive team assumes that data management is purely an IT problem being proactively managed by the IT department - like taking your car in for a basic service and assuming the mechanic will automatically fix the wheel alignment.

You'll notice that some points above concern the CIO or head of IT. This person is usually part of the organisation's executive leadership group and is the key link between business and IT management. Obviously, if the CIO is unfamiliar with data management and its challenges, the rest of the executive will likely be unaware too, and you probably can't rely on the CIO to advocate for you.

It shouldn't be surprising that even if your CIO isn't particularly familiar with data management as a discipline, they may have detailed experience with some parts of it. For example, the CIO may have comprehensive knowledge of data modelling or database design, but know nothing about other components such as business intelligence or data architecture. And unfortunately, without support from the CIO, any plans to establish a data management practice will likely fail.

Within an organisation, the CIO role is highly coveted. To get the CIO job, a person probably has to be ambitious and strategic, and once in the role, they will want to succeed and consolidate their reputation to progress further.

Consider the attributes that lead to the selection of a new or replacement CIO. Experience suggests they generally fall into one of three main categories:

- A long-serving IT department employee who knows how to maintain the IT systems, i.e., a "steady-state" CIO.
- Someone with a track record of running significant projects that have delivered benefits to the organisation in terms of customer service delivery or platform change, i.e., a "new initiative" CIO.
- Someone capable of presenting themselves as an agent of change who is eager to prove themselves by quickly delivering something valuable to the organisation, i.e., an "entrepreneur" CIO.

As a result, any new CIO will likely focus on delivering visible value as soon as possible to cement their selection. This new value may be delivered through new applications, interfaces, or platforms (e.g., a migration to the cloud), or through cost efficiencies and savings. It is most likely that such a CIO would have been selected based on their track record of delivering new capability to the organisation, rather than having a background in data management.

The challenge for the aspiring data management enthusiast is to sell data management to the CIO and demonstrate its ability to avert disasters. This will be addressed in subsequent chapters of this book.

Management don't understand the risks to their data

At its core, data management is all about managing the risks associated with an organisation's data. One can look at the DMBOK with its breakdown of data management into various domains and see WHY each data management domain is important for risk management.

The following table shows some typical risks that exist where a data management component isn't being adequately performed:

DMBOK domain	Risk being mitigated by proper data management
Data Architecture	Data is not structured and organized to allow its use for multiple purposes. Data storage may be growing at an unacceptable rate without consideration of its handling costs.
Data Modelling & Design	Data isn't properly defined so it's not clear what something means or even that the right data was collected from a customer. System enhancements become expensive because data has been organised in a way that is inconsistent with reality.
Data Storage & Operations	Data isn't always available when and where required, so customer service is impacted.
Document & Content Management	Documents that are created by, or initiate business processes get lost and so evidence trails are broken.
Metadata Management	Data moves through the organisation, but it gets transformed and its meaning becomes confused or lost.
Data Quality	Data is becoming progressively corrupt and may become unfit for purpose. Data may lead to AI producing the wrong outcomes.
Data Security	Data can leak from the organisation resulting in massive fines or compensation.
Reference & Master Data Management	There are multiple repositories of the same business information, eg customer details, and it is not clear which data is correct or the most accurate.
Data Integration & Interoperability	Data isn't handled or stored in consistent way and so can't be shared between systems.

DMBOK domain	Risk being mitigated by proper data management
Data Warehousing & BI	Data analysis produces the wrong conclusion. Strategic business decisions are based on wrong data.
Data Governance	Database changes are deployed that break existing Production applications. Data is used for inappropriate/illegal purposes. Data is not protected against the real-world problems that threaten the business.

Business don't understand that it's THEIR data

For many decades, organisations assumed that the IT department had full responsibility for the organisation's data. The CIO was seen as having ultimate authority over the data and therefore must be managing it appropriately. Business involvement with data tended to be reactive to IT requests.

More recently, there has been broad recognition that business users actually own the data, and they can't simply assume that their IT department is managing their data in a way that meets their specific needs. Business now needs to have a strategic view of how enterprise data should be exploited now and in the future.

If your organisation doesn't have someone outside IT accountable for its data, it's likely to be harder to get the business (who hold the purse strings) to allocate funds to data management activities.

Fortunately, we've recently seen Chief Data Officer roles becoming more commonplace, so hopefully we are experiencing a progressive acceptance of business ownership of data.

On the positive side, your organisation is probably full of very capable people who just happen to know little about their data in general and data management in particular. Initial discussions about these topics will likely take them out of their comfort zones, however once they become more educated about the data, associated risks, and possible mitigations, they can become powerful supporters.

Competition for IT resources

A limited IT budget means that improvements to your data management capability must compete with improvements to business- or customer-facing applications and other key infrastructure.

Only in the largest organisations have I seen IT departments with a discretionary budget for data management improvements. Successful data management teams have leveraged past development or operational problems to demonstrate how better data management could have avoided them.

If your organisation has previously experienced a data problem that created a larger business problem, you can leverage this to demonstrate that better data management will save money. In one organisation, we had carte blanche to fix data governance problems after the agency submitted multiple regulatory documents to the government reporting substantially different customer numbers. After the agency head was scrutinized for inconsistent reporting, there was strong support for implementing data governance controls over management reporting.

One feature of IT in the government sector is unspent budget. No department wants unspent budget at the end of the year, because the Department of Finance may decide that if the money isn't needed this year, they can decrease next year's allocation also.

A canny data manager will have several backup proposals ready. If it's discovered that you will underspend your IT budget, you can use one or more of these proposals to spend the available funds. This helps your boss while improving your data management capability.

When your data management problem seems overwhelming

Sometimes you'll find yourself in an organisation where data management standards and processes are almost non-existent. The organisation survives only because talented people do the right thing based on their experience, not because of documented procedures. Because there's no formal data governance policies or procedures, you're relying on professionals implementing their own personal processes. If people change jobs, these processes may no longer be performed.

Sometimes you live in fear of key technical staff leaving or retiring. You know that releases only go smoothly because someone on your team runs a totally undocumented, 20-step process that only they understand.

If you work in an environment like this, it's unsurprising that you'll find the prospect of fixing your organisation's data management problems overwhelming. However, the good news is that many opportunities exist for improvement, which will in turn improve your reputation if you only fix a few of them. A good strategy is to start fixing, improving, or documenting processes and then make sure that others know that you're adding value. Key to this is developing a plan for what you'll work on first.

There is no silver bullet

The term "silver bullet" refers to a mythical bullet that could slay a werewolf, but in a software context it could be seen as a software package that magically solves an IT or business problem.

It is not uncommon for vendors to promote data management solutions suggesting that the answer to data management problems, such as data governance, metadata management, etc, simply involves installing and using their product suite. Unfortunately, this can mislead people about how to fix the underlying deficiencies, potentially worsening the situation.

Brooks' Law states that "adding manpower to a late software project makes it later" [2]. Similarly, installing a new software package may compound your data management problems. Instead of addressing skill, process, or other governance issues, the team may become distracted by populating a software package, assuming this will magically solve existing problems. Furthermore, setting up and operating the new tool may consume scarce data management resources and require additional resources to maintain it.

Product demonstrations are designed to showcase products in a positive light, but they can also obscure the effort required to make them useful. I've seen many sales demonstrations begin with the data management tool already pre-loaded with a comprehensive set of test data, making it appear capable of solving almost any data management problem. The demonstrations sometimes show:

- All the key data assets of the firm, with the ability to drill-down and view database structures and all the table and column metadata including descriptions.
- Data stewards and custodians assigned to all the data assets
- A full data lineage from operational database through to data warehouse showing all data transformations that take place

[2] Frederick P. Brooks, Jr. *The Mythical Man-Month.* 1995 [1975]. Addison-Wesley.

- Impact analysis showing the full organisational impact of database changes from original database through to final BI reports that are dependent upon that particular column.
- Automatic identification of all personally-identifiable information (PII) held within the organisation's databases, such as credit card details, social security numbers, and name and address data.

The above points look great in a well-planned product demonstration and can give the impression that purchasing the tool will deliver the same level of data governance control. However, while the tool may offer excellent data management integration and useful functionality, it can gloss over the effort and resources needed to collect and maintain all this data. Consider the effort required to:

- Gain access to every key Production database and organize access by the tool so it can reverse-engineer the database structure. Find all the table and column descriptions for your legacy databases.
- Identify all data integration paths and repositories that hold all the data transformations being made by the integration software
- Identify the business data stewards responsible for every database or business facet of the data (eg a database may hold both customer data, sales data, product data, and manufacturing data all of which have separate data steward relationships)

Data management tools can certainly benefit an organisation, but you must be prepared to allocate the necessary resources to populate them.

While tools can't assist in getting business buy-in and support for data stewards, they make recording and publishing data much easier.

So, while data management tools may seem appealing and like the answer to your data management problems, they rarely address the organisational issues that are causing your current data management deficiencies.

The good news

The good news is that your organisation and colleagues are unlikely to be averse to data management. It's more likely they've never had the time to understand it. They'll understand many of the components individually, but they've probably never been exposed to data management as a discrete discipline that manages these components in an integrated fashion.

In my experience, organisations rarely show animosity towards data management. Instead, they're often surprised it exists. The DMBOK is a significant selling point here because it proves its maturity as a discipline. Its presence means you don't have to justify the concept and can shape all future discussions around it.

Recap

Establishing data management capability means you need to confront and mitigate the business realities likely to block your attempts to implement and enforce policies, procedures, and standards.

Potential blockers include:

- the modern IT environment, expected to deliver more with less budget, will require convincing before allocating resources for data management.
- management's lack of understanding of data management and its benefits for the organisation will require education.
- management's lack of understanding of tangible business risks resulting from data loss or compromise will also require education.
- the business's assumption that IT is solely responsible for data management and adequately protecting data, which is often unfounded.
- competition with application development teams for scarce resources, requiring the wider IT community to understand that investments in data management will yield future benefits.
- the perceived overwhelming number of data management deficiencies, leading to reluctance to investigate or commit to solutions.

- vendors offering data management tools that promise complete solutions, potentially distracting management from addressing the root causes of problems.

Most blockers can be mitigated by educating both management and your IT peers on the scope of data management, as promoted by DMBOK. This document can introduce data management concepts to the organisation and highlight the benefits of managing disparate data activities under a single framework.

PLANNING YOUR DATA MANAGEMENT JOURNEY

The previous chapter should have given you a better understanding of how your data management capability is perceived within your organisation's broader business environment and IT department. Hopefully, you now have a clearer picture of the obstacles you need to overcome.

While the previous chapter introduced many potential problems, this chapter will outline strategies to address them. We'll also identify techniques for establishing and sustaining a data management practice for the long term.

In tandem with addressing data management obstacles, you can begin building capability and recognition—there's no need to proceed sequentially. Removing obstacles can take time, and some may only be resolved once your colleagues see your data management practice in action.

Being clear about the objectives

From a high-level perspective, we need to be clear about the strategic objectives you'll need to achieve a sustainable data management capability:

- Getting support from the Executive team
- Getting support from your IT department
- Getting support from the rest of your organisation
- Showing that you have a feasible plan
- Demonstrating that you are delivering something of value

Keep these points in mind, because most of what we do should be targetted at delivering one or more of these objectives. While this list might appear daunting at first, you will likely find that once you start developing relationships and identifying the more urgent data management problems being experienced, you'll also be progressing the delivery of these objectives.

The following sections address your organisation's data management from a first-principles approach and will hopefully give you an insight to how you can approach identifying your data management needs and the planning process.

Who wants data management and why?

At DAMA meetings, after people present their latest data management initiative or success, I often hear questions about how they got corporate support for their data management practice. This seems to be a primary blocker for most people, because they feel no support for introducing new practices or procedures.

The most important guidance I can give here is that introducing data management will be most successful if it is driven top-down and not bottom-up. You are seen implementing processes because the Executive or senior management wants them, not because you personally believe your organisation needs it. Things roll downhill faster than you can roll them up hill.

Ideally, corporate decision-makers need to instruct the rest of the organisation that the data must be managed professionally and not as a by-product of normal operations. Sometimes this may result in a direction expressed to the CIO of your organisation while in other cases it might result in something more significant.

So, what would prompt the Executive to consider a data management solution? The answer is RISK.

Generally, the larger an organisation gets the more risk-averse the executives become, because the consequences for the organisation become greater. The consequences for the executives personally also become bigger – in today's business environment being seen as responsible for a major data breach could be career-ending.

You're more likely to get the Executive to consider support for data management if you can expose risks to the organisation, and possibly to them personally, if the data isn't being managed properly.

Planning your assault on the Executive

We've said that getting the Executive to drive or at least support the introduction of a data management practice is crucial. Unfortunately, there's no standard roadmap on how to initiate such a dialogue with the Executive.

However, I've seen a few effective plans of attack that are generally applicable and may work for you.

The most common approach is via the CIO, who is generally part of the Executive. It is difficult, and perhaps career-limiting in most organisations, to bypass your boss. The challenge here is getting the CIO to sponsor your approach to the rest of the Executive, and I've found support when the CIO does not want to be the person to set the enterprise priorities because they recognise that some of the policies need to be whole-of-organisation ones and not IT-imposed. Ideally, the CIO will become your sponsor for further discussion with the Executive.

One example I've used for this whole-of-organisation policy was to request guidance about what data risks the organisation was prepared to accept and which risks they wanted me to mitigate. As part of this discussion, I needed guidance about whether our data needed to be protected from a natural disaster that destroyed our city – at the time, both our primary and secondary data centres were only miles apart. The CIO recognised that this was not a decision that could be made by the IT department alone, so sponsored a direct discussion with the rest of the Executive.

A second approach is via existing governance structures. Some organisations have a form of high-level data or information sub-committee that reports to the Executive. This committee is likely to be amenable to the promotion of data management practices, and they may be able to facilitate direct discussions with the Executive.

An alternative to this exists if your organisation has a Chief Data Officer. Generally, this role is outside of IT and is responsible for making policy decisions about the organisation's data. This person can be approached as a possible supporter of data management as they will likely be keen to be involved in any discussion that involves the enterprise's data – especially for discussions on any Executive requirements.

Before you undertake any direct marketing activities with the Executive, it will be extremely beneficial to assess who may already be onside and who might need more persuasion. You may even be able to get individual executives to help with this assessment. At one organisation I was extremely surprised at the amount of support that I got from the CFO – I had assumed he was somewhat distant from the data landscape, but it turned out he was very interested in any inefficiencies and problems with our IT solutions that caused projects to overrun or maintenance costs to be higher than we preferred.

Selling data management to the Executive

You can't tell the Executive that they need data management. You have to sell the idea the same way a salesman sells a product. Most often, this means first getting the customer to recognise that they have a problem and then selling them a product or service that will remove their problem and make their life easier. It's the same with data management – you are going to have to:

- do some research and identify what data problems and potential risks the organisation or key stakeholders have
- get senior management, or ideally the Executive, to acknowledge that they have these problems
- explain that data management can help alleviate these problems
- sell them a solution based upon the introduction of a data management practice

The "elevator pitch"

The concept of having an elevator pitch is quite mature and there's popular support for them being a successful tool in gaining executive support. So, what is an elevator pitch?

> Imagine you are in an elevator with the CIO or some other important member of the Executive team. You've got their total attention for maybe one minute. What do you say to them in that minute that will get their interest and support?

There are many theories of what works and what doesn't; however there doesn't seem to be any proven technique. After all, what manager is going to admit that a strategic direction changed because of a 60-second sales pitch in an elevator?

If we take the elevator pitch as a microcosm of a potentially longer dialogue, then what is likely to work? Would your Executive team be swayed by a 60-second discussion of data management, or a complaint that you didn't have enough resources, or that you weren't being involved in the right planning meetings? Would you get their immediate interest by discussing the data backup strategy you are working on?

It's unlikely – they're more likely to get out on an earlier floor just to get away from you.

But what will get their attention is a talk about a business risk that is meaningful to them, a risk that may also be a potential enterprise problem, or a risk that the person didn't even realise they were responsible for.

Instead of discussing something potentially boring (to the person) like data backups, perhaps you could re-frame it as a lament about not being clear about what types of data loss your organisation needs to defend itself against. Can you pique their interest by saying there's no organizational guidance about whether you need to protect the data against a natural disaster (you can insert here some type of disaster common in your area like hurricanes or floods)? Ideally. you want the elevator pitch to result in an invitation to discuss the issue in more detail or a request to help the Executive identify if they have a problem that's not being addressed and that maybe they could be blamed for not mitigating.

The key thing about elevator pitches is that you need to have them thought out in advance, rather than trying to craft them on-the-fly. It's worth spending some time identifying one or more key/important business problems that you are trying to help the organisation solve that will obviously require some executive input. Test the pitch out against someone outside your data management team and see if it resonates or is still boring.

Getting the Executive to recognise their data risks

Members of the Executive likely have the assumption that the IT department is doing all the right things to manage the organisation's data. Possibly your organisation has never experienced a data disaster, so people haven't ever really considered the potential consequences of such disasters. People often begrudge the cost of insurance until they have a major disaster and then are glad that they have it.

> I once regretted taking out a new-for-old replacement insurance option for a new car purchase. Soon after, someone ran into me and did a massive amount of damage – I was really pleased when the insurance company rang me and asked if I wanted my car fixed or just replaced with a new one.

Good data management is like insurance for your data. Consequently, people often question whether they need it, or what options are worth paying for – everyone wants to pare it down to the bare minimum. The key challenge is to ensure senior management understand the consequences of various disasters that might impact their data.

One particularly good thing about the DMBOK is that it brings together the major data-related functions under a single data management umbrella. Previously, these functions were scattered across your IT landscape and not managed cohesively. The existence of DMBOK means you don't have to try and convince people about what constitutes data management – there is a large tome you can wave in front of people that documents a comprehensive industry standard. Over the years, I've discovered that most IT people are good corporate players – if you present an industry or corporate standard to them, they are happy to follow it rather than dispute it. As a result, you are less likely to get disagreement about what constitutes data management.

So, having established the scope of data management, how do you get the Executive to recognise their data risks? Here, you need some knowledge about your business and the industry it operates in. Risk mitigation is most effective when it is personal – ideally, you want the members of the Executive to see that data risks impact them professionally or even personally. Different people may care about different risks, so you may need to cast your net widely.

We'll address data risks in more detail later, but let's take a common IT data function and see how it can be presented within an enterprise risk framework rather than just as "something that the IT folks do". We'll use data backups as an example.

Example: data backup

Almost everyone these days is aware of the need for backups, even if they're not an IT professional. Anyone who's ever written a document and had it corrupted or accidentally deleted knows that you need to keep backups. The Executive rightly expects the IT department to be backing up their organisation's data as just one of those "things that the IT folks do".

But what risk are you actually protecting against?

If you're working on an assignment or writing a report on a laptop, you might keep previous versions of the document. If you mess up or corrupt the current document, you can revert to the previous version stored in a folder on your laptop.

But does that protect you if the laptop is stolen or the laptop drive fails? No. So, you might introduce another component to your backup solution – keeping a copy on a separate backup disk in your apartment.

But does that protect you against someone breaking into your apartment and stealing both your laptop and your backup disk? No. So, you need another component to your backup solution if you want to protect yourself against that specific threat.

It's the same when we look at corporate data. We need to know what risks the data needs to be protected from – is it just accidental deletion, disk drive failure, loss of the data centre itself, loss through ransomware, or even loss of a city (say, in the event of a large natural disaster).

Backups are traditionally done by IT, but when framed as mitigation for business risks, it is the Executive that needs to identify the risks they want the data to be protected against. Some mitigations can be cheap, while others can be expensive, and it's hard to get support for an expensive solution unless it meets a need explicitly identified by the Executive.

Risks also need to be considered from the perspective of their resulting consequences. A student losing a document will have to spend valuable time re-creating the paper. But what are the consequences of an organisation losing its customer data, or the industrial secrets it holds? When discussing the possible data risks with the Executive, you need them to recognise the potential consequences of the organisation losing various types of data. Some losses could cause minor annoyances, while others could result in a combination of extreme reputational damage, litigation, and replacement of the organisation's head.

Therefore, when discussing this with the Executive, one of the first questions you should ask them is: "What risks do **you** want us to protect the data against?"

Other risks

Some risks, like the data loss as described above, are relatively straightforward to discuss with executives – the causes and ramifications can be clearly elaborated.

However, when you consider all the sectors of the DAMA wheel, you will see that the organisation is exposed to other risks if any of the domains are not being adequately managed.

The following table identifies some of the risks taken by an organisation when not managing a particular data management domain to an adequate standard.

Domain	Possible Business Risk
Data architecture	We don't know what data we have. We don't know which of our systems is creating or changing what data. We are creating islands of data that can't be re-used. We don't know if we are meeting regulatory requirements for our data.
Data design	We don't know what our data means. We aren't storing our data logically so we're likely to regularly need to restructure it or create fragile patches.
Data operations	We aren't protecting our data, and it could be lost or stolen.

Domain	Possible Business Risk
	Our reputation could be severely damaged. Our business could fail. Our systems slow down when busy and restrict customer service.
Data integration	We can't share our data with internal or external applications. Important data gets stale or inconsistent with other data.
Master data management & reference data	We hold differing facts for the same customer and we're not sure which is most correct. When we're advised that some externally-sourced data (eg customer address) is incorrect we have to make the same change in multiple systems rather than just doing it once.
Business intelligence	Our BI reports provide bad information, impacting both tactical and strategic decision-making.
Metadata management	We don't know how some business facts are being calculated and what data the calculations were based on.
Document management	We can't find documents when we need them, so we don't have evidence to support our decisions. Customers call us about letters they've received but we're not sure what we sent them.
Data quality	Our data can't be relied upon to be accurate, and our databases suffer from data cancer that may not be detected until too late. Routine batch processes fail because of data problems.
Data governance	Data is changed without adequate control or visibility. The wrong data is provided to external stakeholders. We fail an audit of our data processes. We fail to meet regulatory requirements.

When discussing risks with the Executive, the consequences need to reflect a significant business impact. There can be a tendency to state a consequence and assume that the potential impacts to the business are self-evident. However, nothing could be further from the truth – sometimes you have to guide a person to the point where they can articulate the business impact, or even a personal impact.

Here's an example that shows that something that is a significant business problem for one organisation isn't a problem for another.

> I worked at one organisation where bad customer postal addresses resulted in physical mail being returned - creating significant additional work handling the received mail, contacting the customer and correcting the address, and then re-sending new mail. Reporting that 5% of our customer addresses were bad would cost us millions of dollars per year, so everyone in the organisation understood that poor address data quality was "bad".
>
> In contrast, at another organisation we interacted with our customers almost exclusively online, and rarely did we ever physically post anything to them. Telling a senior manager that we had bad customer postal addresses would result in a shrug and a change of topic because it had almost no business impact.

Capitalising on this knowledge, you need to present risks that have a significant impact on the finances or reputation of the organisation. Don't just assume that every risk will be given equal importance and that every risk has a business impact.

Locking in executive support

Previously, we've looked at getting the Executive to recognise there are data risks that need to be managed to avoid future problems. However, we want to achieve more than a once-off commitment to an urgent data management need; we want a recognition that a long-term commitment is necessary.

The DMBOK

Another step to be achieved is getting the organisation to recognise data management as a distinct discipline within IT, and ideally, the need to empower a dedicated data management team. This work is likely already underway if you are seen carrying around a copy of the DMBOK book or you feature parts of the DMBOK in any presentation that you've given. This proves to everyone that data management exists as a discipline and it isn't just a result of your personal enthusiasm.

The DMBOK is particularly useful in shaping your discussions with management. You can use its breakdown of data management into discrete functional areas to address your organisation's data management weaknesses or problems. Using a Body of Knowledge means you don't have to come up with, or justify, any such breakdown – you can have the confidence that you are following industry best practice.

Another weapon in your data management arsenal is the concept of a Certified Data Management Professional (CDMP). People without direct data management experience are probably unaware that such a certification exists and, as a result, haven't considered the implications. If you were to investigate your organisation's finance department, I'm sure you will find it full of certified accountants and CPAs – there's recognition that finance should be run by people with appropriate certification for the work that they do. A similar analogy can be drawn with data management – you can pose the question: "Is our data being managed by appropriately qualified data management professionals?". Your finance director will likely understand the ramifications of such a question.

In summary, there is a need to get your organisation to understand that for data management:

- a Body of Knowledge already exists that is mature and ongoing
- staff can be trained in the Data Management Body of Knowledge and become certified practitioners
- corporate risks and liabilities can be reduced when appropriately certified staff follow industry standard practices.

Looking for opportunities to support – Disaster Recovery

You should always look for opportunities to support the organisation via a data management approach. Of course, it's not possible to predict what specific requirements may exist, but the objective here is to be seen applying a data management approach to help solve a need.

One example I'll put forward is IT disaster recovery. This is often coupled with the concept of business continuity, and sometimes these two get squashed together – so you may need to use a data management framework in any discussions to avoid stepping on other teams' toes.

For this example, I'll use the following concepts:

- Disaster recovery (DR) is a process that is formally initiated by an organisation following a significant IT failure that requires extraordinary processes and decision-making to restore the required services. Disaster recovery cannot be achieved under a business-as-usual regime and may require some services to be paused or terminated in order to restore others, and as a result, is likely to require Executive authority.
- Business continuity (BC), sometimes called business continuity management (BCM), encompasses the plans and processes established for an organisation to continue operations in the case of a disaster, IT-related or otherwise. This can include physical and biological disasters as well as IT problems, for example, a virulent virus outbreak or a structural or infrastructure problem affecting the building.

Disaster recovery is a good example because most organisations need to plan for it, and it is difficult for people to oppose establishing the organisation's risk tolerances and expectations.

Large organisations often have a business continuity management team of some sort that is part of the greater business governance organisation. However, these teams often haven't identified risks and potential disasters that might be recognizable only to the IT team. For example, the physical loss of a data centre and loss of communications **to** a data centre are two separate risks that may require quite different mitigations, even though they appear to have the same impact on business processes.

As a result, it is reasonable to suggest that a data management team should coordinate the planning for data-oriented disasters and the recovery from them. This can be pitched as assisting an existing BCM team with their contingency planning and also the IT department being proactive in meeting the needs of the organisation.

You may be questioned about why this is a "data management" responsibility, and this is a fair question. In my experience, the data of an organisation includes both the executable software as well as the business data itself, and the software needs to be redundantly pre-positioned and backed up just like the business data, so the data management umbrella seems to cover the lion's share of the problem. When we perform backups, we usually back-up not just the business data but the deployed software as well. It may be useless to back up a database if we don't have software that can actually use that version of the database design.

Assisting with other corporate obligations

Sometimes there are opportunities to be seen as valuable by assisting the organisation with other problems. Often these aren't highly visible, and you may first have to get the CIO to recognise that the problem exists. Then it's a matter of explaining how you can help the CIO and the rest of the organisation mitigate the risk. Part of the sales strategy here is to frame these problems as data management risks that need to be managed as part of a data management framework. The other part of the strategy is that once you've convinced the customer that they have a problem, you offer to solve it for them. Some examples of these unrecognised problems include:

- GDPR compliance – what impact if any does this have on your data holdings? If you offer services to the EU, can you meet their data obligations?
- Are you publishing data that you might need to redact if requested, such as someone's personal contact details? If so, what is the process to be followed?
- Do you know what datasets contain personally-identifiable information?
- What are your data retention requirements? Are there any regulatory requirements that must be met? Is there data that is being retained that is actually a financial risk, eg copies of personal data that is no longer required and if leaked may cause a huge financial penalty?
- Do you have multiple copies of data hanging around that may not be up-to-date?

Who's responsible for the data?

Throughout this chapter we've looked at what we can do to create a perceived need for data management within the Executive as a way of getting support and funding for data management initiatives.

Another useful way of gaining some Executive support is to use the functional breakdown of the DAMA wheel in the DMBOK and to encourage others to view the management of data through this lens. A simple example of the power of the DMBOK is to look at who is responsible for what.

I once had a session explaining the DMBOK concepts with one of an organisation's senior executives. She was pleased to see a formal decomposition of data management that she could rely on. I'd been reviewing each of the segments of the DAMA wheel and explaining what each involved.

Our organisation's glaring gap in data management came as a result of her initial questions: "Who's responsible for data security?" and "Who's responsible for data quality?". I then had to explain that there was no-one in the organisation with specific responsibility for the security of the organisation's data. Sure, there were plenty of cybersecurity folks ensuring our systems and networks were secure, but there was no-one specifically tasked with responsibility for ensuring that the data security practices of the DMBOK were being met for our corporate data. From an executive's perspective, it was clear that she wanted somebody who owned the problem of securing the corporate data, and someone who was able to report on the security requirements and processes in place. At the time, our IT security was mainly infrastructure- and architecture-focused and didn't have any particular focus on corporate data.

Similarly, regarding data quality, it was clear that no-one specifically had overall ownership, and while there were business systems with clear owners, there were no processes established that reported to her on the quality of the organisation's data. Again, the data management lens suggested that there should be a person and process available to manage and report on data quality.

While the take-up of the DMBOK created a lot of work, I counted it as a success that the DMBOK's simple decomposition of data management into simple-to-understand functional areas made it usable by non-data people as a method of both understanding the scope of data management and providing a road map of how to identify weaknesses and remedial actions.

Getting support from the rest of your organisation

Getting support from the Executive is a big plus, but it's also necessary for you to get support from the rest of your organisation, particularly the IT department. There are several reasons for this:

- Data management activities generally involve the use of resources from other teams, and you want these teams to make the resources available
- You want the other IT teams to see you as delivering value so that they support your proposed activities and do not white-ant your efforts
- You want them to identify data management problems that they see or are experiencing

Who are your likely allies?

Superficially, your allies are likely to be the teams that have some operational responsibility for managing the organisational data. An organisation usually falls into one of the following categories, and this will impact where you need to seek allies.

- The organisation has a mature data management team that has broad responsibility over corporate data
- The organisation has no existing data management team, and the data management functions are distributed across multiple IT teams
- The organisation has a data management team with responsibility for some functions, with others managed by other teams

If your organisation is in the latter two, then potentially influential teams that you need to seek support from include:

- Architecture
- Database design

- Records management
- IT Security
- Business continuity/disaster recovery
- DBA/database operations
- Project management office

For each team that you want to engage with, you need to identify what's in it for them. If there's no benefit to them then they aren't likely to support your team or your activities.

It is important to work with each team to understand what part of the data management puzzle they are responsible for and what problems they have. In some cases, they may be unaware of their own limitations and risks and are simply doing things the way they've always done things without considering ever-improving industry best practices.

It can be useful to identify ways that a data management team can alleviate these problems. Maybe there are things that they'd like to do but have never actually put into practice as a result of priorities and their own limited resources.

It's not possible to predict what potential data management shortfalls may exist for your organisation, but the following examples may provide some ideas.

Team	Possible Data Management Shortfall
Architecture	• What datastores actually exist that contain corporate data • What data is being transferred to other organisations • Where do we duplicate data • How does data flow between all our systems

Team	Possible Data Management Shortfall
Database design	• Database design standards • Naming standards for cloud data resources • What data needs comprehensive design and what doesn't
Records management	• Identifying data stores with Personally Identifiable Information (PII) • Identifying data retention & disposal requirements for corporate datastores
IT Security	• Identifying mission-critical datastores • Identifying security requirements for each corporate datastore • Reviewing adequacy of data change audit records

Recap

This is a rather long chapter that focuses primarily on planning and deciding how you are going to approach establishing a data management practice.

While the previous chapter discussed the potential blockers that you might experience, this chapter provides some suggestions about how you can overcome them. The key blockers will be business issues rather than technical, so we addressed the human and organisational aspects of the likely resistance.

The first part of the planning process is to understand the Executive team and other senior people that you'll need to get onside if you want to get support to move forward. You'll have to identify who you can work through to access the decision-makers.

You'll also need to work out how you are going to get their interest once you can speak with them. It's usually no good trying to discuss any intricacies of data management – you'll need to focus on business issues that have a real or potential impact on their roles.

- You should prepare an "elevator pitch" in advance to make the most of any casual or unplanned access to someone you want to influence.
- An important way to get senior management's attention is to address risks to the organisation. Risk gains attention, and some organisations have a specialised risk management committee. While risks usually relate to the organisation overall, they can also imply a more personal risk to one or more of the Executives.

A good way of addressing risk is to use the DMBOK as a framework, identifying potential risks resulting from each of the 11 domains. It can be worthwhile assessing each domain in advance to identify how mature your organisation is in each, and any domains that may be potential hotspots for risk. Previously, I gave an example of existing backup processes that may not actually be protecting against real-world threats to the data.

Having got your organisation's interest in data management issues, there's a need to get them invested in the idea that a dedicated data management team might be the best way to manage and report on the many data management risks that may exist. Here, we can leverage the DMBOK to demonstrate that data management is already an industry-recognised discipline with its own practices and standards to rely on.

We also need to sell our expertise as something that can assist with other data-related issues that nobody may have thought about yet. An extension of this is getting clarity about who is accountable for a lot of data issues – for example, who is responsible for your organisation's data quality? How about data security? Data governance? The DMBOK is an invaluable resource for this discussion.

Finally, we looked at your potential allies so that we could identify who they are and start discussions about data problems they might be experiencing and how a data management team could help them.

STARTING FORMAL DATA MANAGEMENT

For this chapter, we'll assume that you have some approval and support to start some sort of formal data management. Congratulations!

Once you have permission to start formal data management, you'll need a plan of attack. There are probably many areas that need attention, but it's easy to get distracted and drawn away from reinforcing the ultimate goal of having data management recognised as a formal discipline within your organisation.

There are two distinct plans that you must create: one is your personal strategy for gaining wider recognition of data management, and the other is a more public plan for the establishment of data management services for the whole organisation. I recommend that you start with the first, as it will help you create the latter, which I will refer to as the data management strategy. These two plans have quite different objectives.

The **recognition plan** will be your personal/internal strategy for getting recognised by different factions in your organisation, like a rock climber finding the narrow cracks in a rock face so they can climb upwards. In a similar fashion, data management needs to be recognised by others, especially other IT folks, as something that is real and something that might make their life easier. Alternatively, they may resonate with the idea that you're doing something that they already recognise is necessary but clearly missing.

Figure 1 - Recognition plan focused on stakeholders

The **data management strategy** is a plan that should ultimately be endorsed by the CIO as a roadmap of the various elements of data management to be established as formal processes. It is important that this strategy resonates with the IT establishment so that they support it and don't resist or stifle it. This is why the recognition plan is so important, because it needs to be the plan for how you gain support and identify the organisation's data management problems you need to solve. A data management strategy isn't very impressive if it can't identify and address the key problems already being experienced.

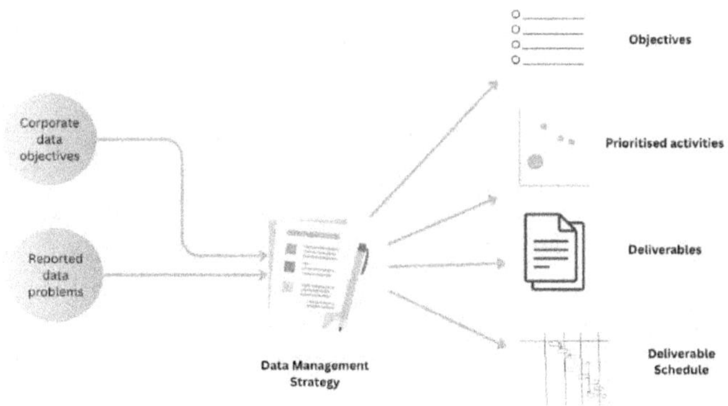

The rest of this chapter will focus on gaining recognition for the data management discipline and developing a strategy that will help you work towards achieving a data management strategy that resonates with the Executive and your peers in IT.

Your plan for gaining recognition

This is the first plan you need to develop to get people to recognise that you exist and you are doing something useful for them and/or the rest of the organisation.

Of course, every workplace is different, and there isn't a one-size-fits-all solution for getting other people to recognise you as a data manager with specific responsibilities. There are, however, some things that you might want to consider:

- Who are important data consumers?
- What problems are they encountering, or what problems that they need a workaround for?
- Are there any communication gaps because no-one is managing the data management arena?

Identify the important data consumers

It is common for people within the IT group to be somewhat unaware of how data is consumed broadly by the rest of the organisation beyond the usual application users. Most people view IT from the perspective of their day-to-day work – some tend only to see the application architecture, others the security architecture or the integration architecture, while some are more focused on the business systems that they support directly.

The following diagram shows a generic business system that is part of a larger overall suite of inter-connected sub-systems. It is typical for each of these sub-systems to have separate maintenance teams and teams that are familiar with that sub-system's data and none of the related downstream data stores. Specifically, the Business Intelligence team may have little or no knowledge of the system-of-record database and any related data quality issues within that system – they may only know about the data that is available in their data warehouse or data lake.

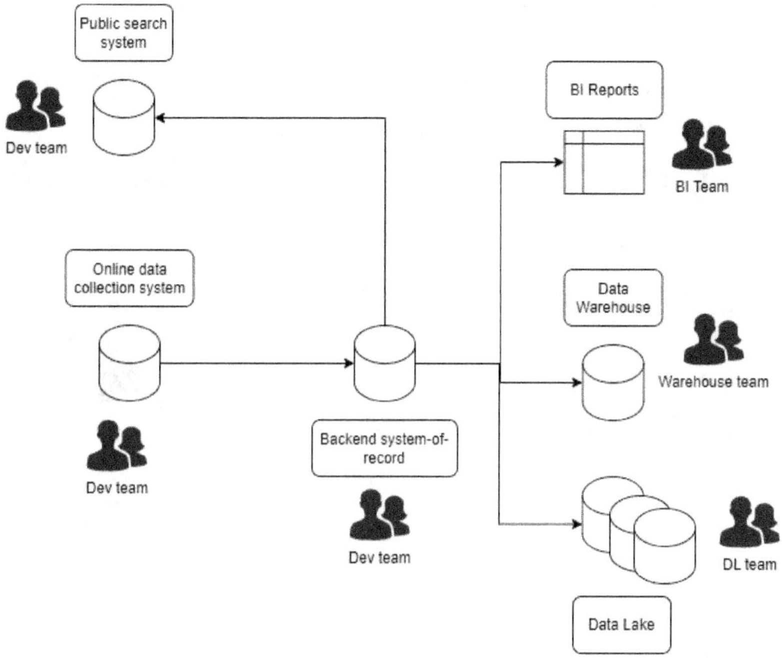

IT development teams tend to view application data as being "owned" by the application. They see an application creating and storing data, maintaining the data, and usually reporting on the data via screens and reports. They may be unaware of the secondary and tertiary data consumers that also use this data, or if they are aware of this, it isn't something they engage with directly because they have no responsibility for it. It's not unusual for data to have an extensive consumption pipeline as it gets used for analysis, business planning, strategic planning, corporate resource planning, and even shareholder or other stakeholder reporting.

Without developing a relationship with these other stakeholders, you are unlikely to fully appreciate all the data management problems that your data creates or could potentially create. Additionally, these stakeholders may appreciate a feedback pipeline that collects their concerns and problems and feeds them back to the IT group. This group of downstream consumers could become powerful allies in your quest for organisational relevance.

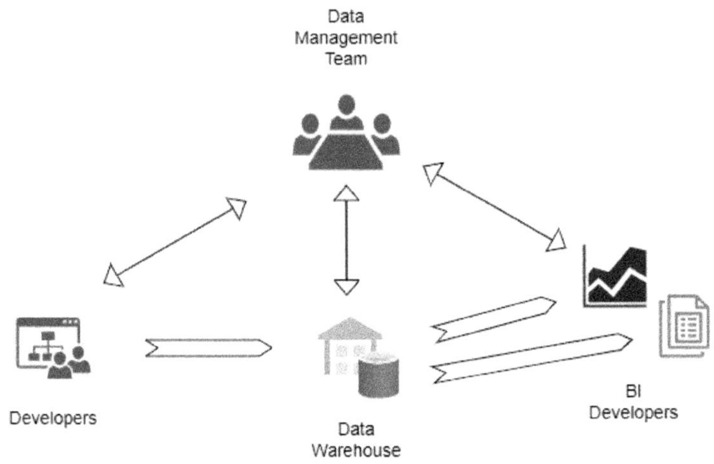

Identify problems that data consumers might be experiencing

There can be significant business risks that flow from the lack of data management coordination. Problems can stem from:

- Data definitions
- Data quality
- Data replication
- Data transformation

The following sections give some examples about how data management gaps can create significant problems or risks for downstream data consumers.

Data definitions

Problems arise if data definitions change and people who rely on them aren't told.

> I once worked in an organisation that recorded people's income. As a result of a policy change, the definition of a person's total income was altered to include fringe benefit income (eg company-supplied car) – which meant that in the following year a significant number of people's recorded income increased without them receiving an actual monetary increase in the real-world.

> We discovered that external policy analysts, who had a great deal of confidence in the accuracy of our data from years of use, were on the verge of officially reporting a significant increase in the national income. When we heard about this, we did some research ourselves and realised that the data analysts were unaware of the change to the definition of *total income*.
>
> It became very evident that we needed better mechanisms to make data definition changes more visible to downstream data consumers. Practically, this could only be delivered as part of an enterprise data management function. At the time, the traditional system development teams had virtually no relationship with the downstream teams that exploited the data.

Data quality

Some data quality problems may not get fixed because they only impact a downstream consumer

Problems with data quality aren't always obvious within the application development and maintenance teams. There can be data problems that don't directly impact application users – and these may get ignored because they don't actually create a problem for the application's business owner.

I have seen an example of this problem related to audit trail data.

> Audit trail data was recorded for a business system mechanically as a by-product of regular business transactions, and regular application users were unaware of this data being recorded because it was part of the underlying, somewhat invisible, "security plumbing" of the system.
>
> This audit trail data was normally only accessed if a security breach was suspected – for example if a hacker was suspected of accessing the network and possibly changing data. Technical documentation about the audit trail was maintained, providing (on paper) assurance that data security requirements are being met.
>
> A routine test activity identified that a recent release caused faulty audit data to be recorded, and a defect was raised. However, the defect was given a low priority because the software developers had more urgent functional enhancements and the business owner was, understandably, more interested in delivering new or improved functionality to users.
>
> The business functional requirements for the system didn't include an audit trail requirement as this had been inherited from the overall security architecture. As a result, it is likely that the business system owner considered the "audit trail problem" was outside their scope and must be the responsibility of some other manager.

> In practice, there wasn't anyone in backlog reviews who was actually responsible for the audit data trail requirement, so the defect remained for a long time.

In this scenario, if IT Security had actually needed to identify any illegal or suspicious activities, the audit trail they expected to rely on may be unusable.

This is an example where an operational data problem didn't get fixed because it only impacted downstream users.

Data replication

Data gets replicated but users don't know that the data is stale or incomplete

Modern system architecture often replicates data to make it more readily available (ie cached) for downstream consumer applications. It is also possible that a cache developed for one application gets reused by another application because it seems easier or faster to access than requesting a new custom cache to be developed.

One downside of this reuse is that it creates a dependency between the two consumers of the cache. The original owner of the cache may decide to make changes to this cache for their own purposes, which can result in the secondary application failing. Changes could include alterations to the subset of data loaded into the cache, transformations being performed as part of the cache population, or even the definition of data made available.

Good data management can help mitigate this risk by publicising the multiple users of the cache, perhaps even vetoing its reuse, and ensuring that all downstream users are aware of proposed changes.

Another risk is the currency of the data in the cache. Consumers might see that a data cache contains the required data because they can view its structure and confirm this. However, what isn't apparent from looking at a physical design is how and when data gets updated. It could be updated incrementally in near real-time whenever data changes in the source database, or it could be updated on a batch schedule. Alternatively, it could be fully deleted and reloaded on schedule or on demand. If the owner of a data cache unilaterally changes its update frequency, it may create significant problems for other systems also using it.

Data management processes can assist with this risk by ensuring that all data stores, including caches, are properly documented.

Data transformation

Data gets transformed as it gets passed on without anyone realizing that the meaning is being changed

Operational data is often exported to operational data stores, data lakes, and data warehouses so it can be consumed by other enterprise users. Accurate metadata is essential for the use of this data because users need to know clearly what data elements mean in order to interpret them correctly.

Furthermore, the data may be transformed by the process to meet some reporting or analysis needs. This new data source must also be documented so that consumers can see what the data means. For example, a new data element might have aggregated some types of personal income to create a new "total earned income" amount; however, it may not be apparent exactly which forms of income have been included, and which have not.

Identify communication gaps relating to data

It isn't uncommon for IT teams to experience communication and coordination problems related to data, especially where a data management team isn't in place. This can occur when development is highly application-based rather than recognizing that data development is also necessary, as outlined in the DMBOK.

The following diagram illustrates how multiple stakeholders are impacted by the development of data solutions. This highlights the need for all stakeholders to receive information about proposed data changes and to be able to provide input to the roll-out schedule for these changes. A Production data definition change may need to be delayed until an important business report that uses that data has been updated to cope with the change.

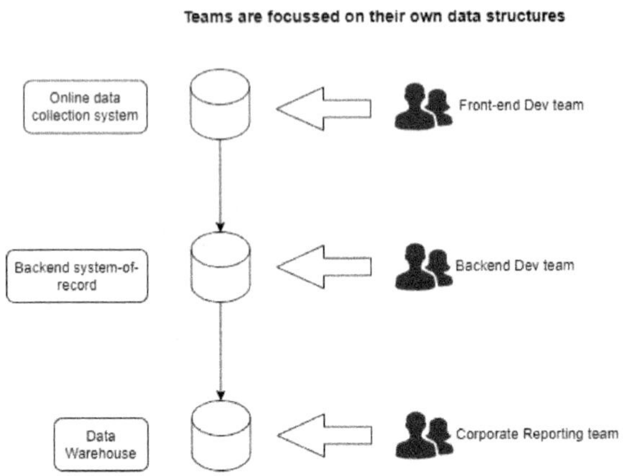

Failure to coordinate upcoming data changes can result in:

- Data sources changes that impact downstream consumer applications and reports failing
- Database outages that cause unplanned outages for dependent applications
- Data definition changes that invalidate existing reports and applications without it being obvious

Data management can significantly improve the change and release process by ensuring there are processes for distributing information about upcoming changes and ensuring that stakeholders have input into key decisions. Downstream users will appreciate advance notifications that allow them to make changes in a timely manner rather than as a reaction to a failure. Conversely, development teams may be unaware that a proposed change to a data structure or its content may create a massive redevelopment task for downstream business intelligence teams.

Avoid being overwhelmed by the size of the task

You may work in a place that seems to have little to no formal data management, and this can be daunting to anyone who wants to build a data management practice. You may be faced with some important questions, like:

- where do I start?
- how am I going to make a visible contribution?

- how can I contribute without a project or resources?

In this scenario, my key recommendation is to avoid getting stuck in the weeds and to focus initially on enterprise-level problems. It is important to gain management recognition and acceptance first, before chasing shop-floor level acceptance, as any guillotine is likely to fall from above.

If we take this approach, then maybe we can re-frame the above questions with a data management perspective to help identify an area where you should focus your attention on initially.

Business Question	Data Management Answer
"where do I start?"	what's the most important data that your organisation has?
"how am I going to make a visible contribution?"	can you identify something that senior management will understand and appreciate?
"how can I contribute without a project or resources?"	what can you do or produce that delivers some value that can be expanded once you have additional resources available.

The first point is the most essential as it will focus you on the key data for the organisation and it allows you to ignore the noise. I'll discuss this further in the following section: *Do you know your data Crown Jewels*?

When you are trying to avoid being overwhelmed by the task, consider the old meme –

Question: "how do you eat an elephant?"
Answer: "one bite at a time"

It's important here to gain some perspective about what you want to achieve. What does your end-state look like? If you don't know this then you won't know which direction to head. Maybe initially you don't even know what the logical end-state should be, perhaps because your organisation is large or complex. In this case, instead of an end-state you set a series of intermediate target-states where you identify a series of achievable goals instead. Once you approach the immediate goal you start refining/clarifying the next.

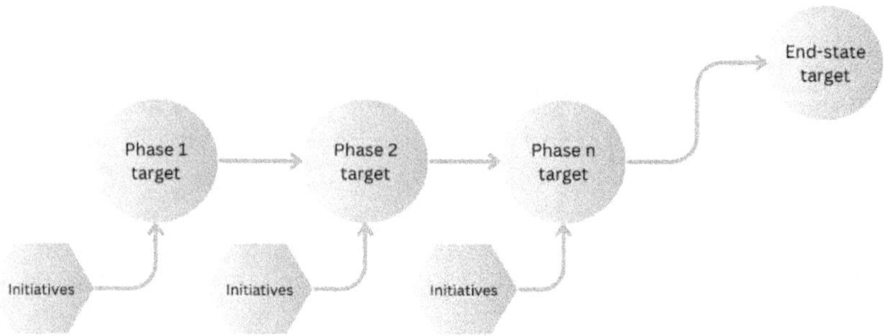

Do you know your data Crown Jewels?

Why define the crown jewels?

If you were to ask your Executive team what your organisation's data "crown jewels" are, you'd probably find that they'd have little difficulty in identifying them. This is because they see the big-picture of your business data and they won't be distracted by a complicated data landscape like a technical person might.

So, what is meant by this term? A quick internet search will return statements like:

- *"The Crown Jewels are the nation's most precious treasures ..."*
- *"If you describe something as someone's crown jewel, you mean it is the most important or valuable thing they have"*

When the term is applied to data, we can infer that the crown jewels refer to the data that is most important to the organization as a whole and not just to one or more parts of it.

If we take a broad enterprise view of these statements, we might re-phrase them more objectively as: "The loss of what data will cause our business to fail?".

If we want a more personal Executive view of our data, we can re-phrase it as: "The loss off what data could ruin my career?"

Surprisingly, it isn't common for organisations to explicitly define their crown jewel data. For many it's assumed to be obvious (although it's not); others may not see the benefits of defining it. As a result, don't be surprised if no-one can give you a pre-defined list of your organisation's crown jewel data.

So why bother defining the data crown jewels? The answer is prioritization.

Why would you worry about, say, the security of timesheet data if the crown jewels were insecure? Shouldn't you ensure that the crown jewels are secure first? This can be a critical first step for establishing enterprise data management.

There are a few quotes, usually attributed to Peter Drucker the legendary management consultant, that are worth repeating here:

- "*Management is doing things right; leadership is doing the right things.*"
- "*What gets measured gets managed*"

Good leadership in data management suggests that you should focus on the most important data before worrying about less-important data. If you don't know what your crown jewels are, then how can you assure senior management that you're managing their most important data?

My intention here is to suggest that if you don't know what your organisation's data crown jewels are, then maybe you can provide some leadership in this area.

This will give you multiple benefits:

1. You have a place to start your data management journey, and
2. You need to interact with the Executive to get their agreement on what constitutes the "crown jewels" and this can reinforce the vision that "these data management folks are doing something useful for us". More on this later.

Defining your crown jewels

The first problem that you might encounter is that what constitutes "critical" or "important' data differs from person to person. The business people (ie the people who perform the main business of your organisation) will usually tell you that their business data is of utmost importance; the finance team will insist that their data is critical; the building security folks will say that the security pass data is critical; the data warehousing people will say that the data warehouse is essential. In other words - everybody believes that their data is essential to the organisation.

> *"All animals are equal, but some animals are more equal than others"*[3].

The challenge is to determine that in a world where all data is important, then what data is the most important? And it's not enough to record that your "HR data" is critical to the organisation – ultimately you need to be able to identify specifically which HR data assets we are talking about. HR data is likely to be a family of datasets and not just one.

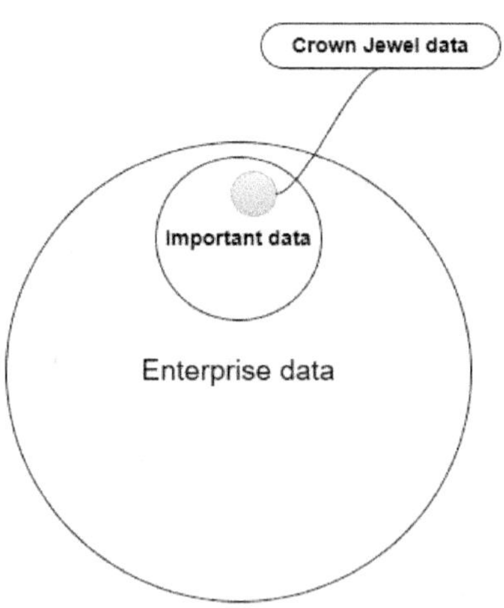

[3] George Orwell, Animal Farm, 1945.

Researching data crown jewels reveals that the term is already a pervasive business concept, but there are different perspectives about what data is included. There are 3 clearly different views expressed, that I'll call *commercial*, *cybersecurity*, and *government.*

The *commercial view* of crown jewels is most likely to focus on the set of data that would most hurt the organisation financially if it were lost. This could be customer data, product stockpile data, intellectual property data, contract data, financial data, data that makes your organisation innovative or unique, or even strategic planning data. If exposure of this to a competitor could destroy your competitive advantage or place in the marketplace, then this is likely part of your crown jewels.

The *cybersecurity view* of crown jewels is most likely more system- and IT-focused rather than revolving around the business data. As a result, it may include datasets related to network and server security, including encryption key, password, and other security configuration data.

The *government view* of crown jewels is the one I've had to deal with the most. These crown jewels relate to data that an agency is required to maintain for legislative or regulatory purposes. For example, a government department that has been established to register motor vehicles and drivers may exist ultimately <u>for no other purpose</u> than to maintain and preserve motor vehicle registration and driver licence data.

So how do you decide what your crown jewel datasets are?

I once saw a suggestion that data managers should be able to "list their crown jewels in 10 seconds with their eyes closed". While I also believe this to be true, if you've never been down this path before it can be challenging to get agreement on what data is actually in this set. Most people have no idea just how much enterprise data their organisation has; they generally only know about the data that they are involved with.

When trying to define one government agency's crown jewels, I first had to define a set of objective criteria by which the crown jewel datasets could be identified. Like anything else that you need to approach from first principles, you also need to get agreement on these principles before delving into the details.

At my agency, we agreed that the core crown jewel criteria were:

- Data that we were legislatively required to maintain
- Data that we were required to maintain under international treaty
- Data necessary for the core functioning of the organisation, eg our document management system, finance data, etc
- Data necessary for maintaining our IT solutions, eg our software source code
- Any other data identified by our organisation's information governance committee that should be included in the crown jewels. Strategically, we included this criterion to avoid conflict when a senior manager insisted on something being included that didn't meet other criteria.

What was our rationale for the above list?

Basically, a loss of any of the above data could result in the failure of our organisation:

- The loss of legislative- or treaty-related data would likely result in the replacement of senior leadership and maybe the dissolution of the agency itself.
- The loss of core operational data would mean that our organisation would no longer be able to operate. Eg what if we lost all our official documents?
- Our IT systems were critical for the services we provided to both our internal and external customers and represented hundreds of millions of dollars of investment. The inability to continue operation and evolution of those systems would mean that our core delivery of services to the public and industry would fail and therefore we could not continue our assigned mission.

An equivalent set of criteria exists for commercial organisations:

- What data are you legally required to maintain?
- The loss of what data would cause your business to fail?
- The loss or exposure of what data could ruin your company financially or reputationally? For example: customer personal data whose leak might result in crippling legal penalties and loss of customer trust.

When deciding on your selection criteria, you must involve the Executive team in the discussions because as "crown jewels" there must be recognition that loss of this data could destroy the organisation. This is not something that can be decided by a data management team, but by some authorised group or committee on behalf of the whole organisation.

Surprisingly, you are likely to find that the Executive don't get caught in the weeds of dataset selection and are likely to have a broad understanding of the data that is critical to the organisation. The CFO will clearly understand and be able to identify the critical financial data. The CEO will be able to identify the critical business data. Similarly, the CIO, CHRO, and COO will be able to identify the data that is critical to their parts of the organisation. None of these people are likely to insist that organisation would be destroyed if the building security pass data were lost - it might be an annoyance, but it could be overcome.

Keep in mind that the Executive will identify the types of data that constitute crown jewels and not identify the specific technical datasets in your infrastructure. This would be a subsequent Data Management responsibility to take the broad direction and then narrow it down to specifics.

Before you start defining the crown jewels

By now you'll have recognised that defining your crown jewels might require a lot of discussion and possibly argument before you get to a final list.

I recommend that you identify in advance who will have ultimate approval - maybe this will be your CEO, a member of the Executive, or even the Chair of some committee.

There is a real risk that you'll need someone to stop further disagreement and make the decision on behalf of the organisation. Fortunately, I've found that senior executives are actually comfortable with this process as their jobs often entail hearing contradicting opinions and making a decision and then getting everyone on-board with the decision.

Using the Crown Jewels for recognition purposes

The previous sections discussed why it is good to have identified your organisation's data crown jewels, and a basic strategy for identifying what makes up this set.

However, another important reason for doing this is to gain Executive recognition about the value of data management.

More specifically, it is important to your data management recognition strategy because:

- If your organisation doesn't currently have a defined set of crown jewels, then delivering this can be a perfect way to demonstrate that Data Management has a beneficial impact on the organisation.
- It demonstrates that Data Management has an organisation-wide view of the data and is therefore best-placed to coordinate work of this nature.
- It provides a vehicle for you to liaise with the Executives and other senior business leaders on enterprise data management and sell your relevance to them.
- It opens the door for subsequent discussions on enterprise-wide discussions, such as what risks this crown jewel data needs to be protected against.
- Because the Executive has defined or approved the set of crown jewels data it provides the opportunity for you to link subsequent work directly with their strategic business requirements.

Recap

This chapter addressed the problem of where you could start formal data management.

Having been given permission to start building some capability, there is a risk that you start working on something that you think is important but isn't seen as particularly important to other teams.

The first challenge is to plan your approach to data management by developing a strategy for getting data management recognised as a valuable IT discipline by other teams. To do this, you need to:

- identify the key data stakeholders in the organisation
- start talking to the other teams and find out what data problems may be impacting their work

- investigate the organisation's data, data flows, and data consumers and look for any apparent problems, such as a lack of documentation or coordination about upcoming changes, and other issues that might impact on the performance of other teams

Next, we looked at a strategy for deciding what data makes up your organisation's crown jewels and how this can be used to prioritize subsequent investigation and analysis. Identifying the crown jewels demonstrates to other teams that you have an enterprise-wide view of the organisation's data, and it's an area where you can demonstrate leadership.

Resulting from these activities, you should now know who the key players are in the data space, what problems they have that can be opportunities for data management, an understanding of what data is critical to the organisation, and where to focus your attention in the short term.

COLLECTING THE DATA MANAGEMENT REQUIREMENTS

Before you can do any real planning for your data management activities, you need to know what you need to build or fix.

Be wary of approaching data management solely from the perspective of an expert who can see what needs to be done. I've been a data architect for a long time, and when I try to explain the data architect role in a particular organisation, I usually fall back to explaining that I do whatever that customer wants me to do. If you want support from those above you and those around you, you need to be satisfying a need that they have – you're less likely to get active support if you are proposing to fix things that they don't care about.

Plan your planning

I'm a veteran of an application development trend called "*rapid application development*". The idea espoused by its supporters, and the inevitable highly paid consultants, was that you'd get a group of stakeholders together in a workshop and quickly prototype a solution that you'd solidify later. It was like an early attempt at agile development, and all the in-vogue vendors were pushing IT tools that supported this process. Unfortunately, we ultimately recognised that this technique was better described as "design in haste and repent at leisure" – as designing quickly often resulted in poor solutions being deployed that cost a lot of effort and money to re-engineer later.

The lesson here is that you shouldn't expect that getting a group of people together in a room to quickly brainstorm an approach won't necessarily result a well-considered strategy.

Good planning requires research and preparation. Getting a group of strangers together in a room to plan a data management strategy is just asking for trouble, and you'll likely end up with a *rapid data management strategy*.

I'd recommend meeting with each stakeholder individually to understand what they do for the organisation, their deliverables, the data they depend on and/or produce, their challenges, their pain points, and any useful background for your data management planning.

Start with a data collection workshop

An effective tool in getting the data stakeholders to be supportive of your strategic planning is to hold a data collection workshop to identify and collect any data-oriented issues that are creating problems, creating unnecessary work, or preventing improvements or innovation. The intention is not to solve any problems, but just to identify the main problems that need to be addressed and their relative urgency.

It is important that the stakeholders get to understand the broad range of problems being experienced across the organisation, otherwise they'll tend to assume that their problems should have priority.

An important side benefit is that it will establish you as an authority figure across the whole enterprise data landscape, and maybe the only one with direction and plan.

Develop your own strawman strategy in advance

If you've invested time in understanding the work of the individual data stakeholders and their pain points, then you are in a good position to direct the workshop in a systematic way, making sure you draw out people's issues.

It can be a good idea to also develop your own strawman strategy and use the workshop to test your understanding and assumptions. However, be prepared to listen to the problems and ideas presented as they might be right and some of your ideas wrong.

An additional benefit of having a strawman approach is that it will help you avoid the old problem of "a camel is a horse designed by a committee". Having thought out a somewhat viable solution in advance you can redirect discussions and decisions that aren't taking you in a successful direction.

Running a data management problem workshop

There are several distinct objectives for this type of workshop:

1. to identify a shared vision with the stakeholders for the outcomes they'd like to achieve by improving data management.

2. to get the stakeholders comfortable with viewing data management, and its deficiencies, from the framework of the DAMA wheel, and

3. to identify the urgent & important data problems that need to be addressed.

Introducing the DAMA wheel

Data management may be a fuzzy concept to some stakeholders, and they are likely to have quite different interpretations of its scope.

To address this, introduce them to the DAMA wheel. DAMA have decomposed data management practice into a series of eleven domains.

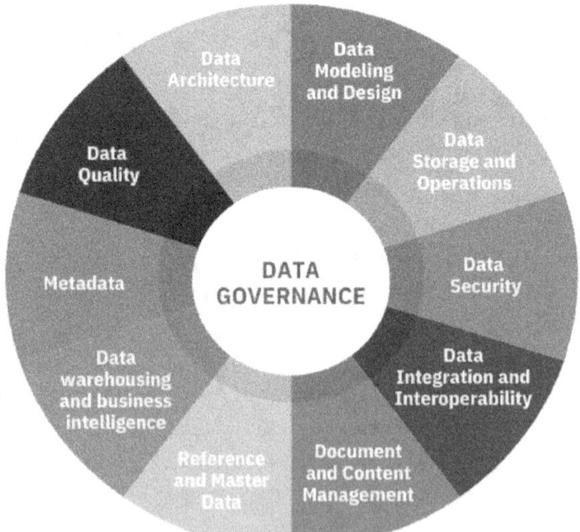

At this stage you probably shouldn't go into too much detail, but it's valuable for people to understand that DAMA has established a mature framework that you will be using to define the scope of data management for the purposes of the workshop.

Because you are using the industry-standard DAMA framework there should be no need to justify this breakdown. You are likely to gain credibility yourself by building on what they should perceive as an established standard.

Be prepared to explain each component of the wheel and the terms that people may not be familiar with. For example, be prepared to explain "master data" and "master data management".

Start with the future data management vision

Achieving a shared vision is much easier if your organisation has an existing data strategy or some form of corporate strategy that identifies the longer-term plan for the use of data. If you don't have one, then you need to identify a set of simple outcomes that would encourage the stakeholders to support you. These will obviously be organisation-specific, but examples could include:

- reducing the number of client support calls that are caused by bad data
- reducing the amount of mail returned because of invalid mailing addresses
- having data of sufficient quality to allow customers to self-service
- having data stored and organised optimally for applications to allow fast interactions
- having customer-facing data available 24x7
- having one master set of customer data rather than multiple systems each holding their own customer data
- providing confidence to the organisation that the data is well protected against cyber threats or physical loss

Your vision should be a high-level statement of business requirements for your data to support your organisation in the future.

Ideally, every activity you subsequently seek to improve should link back to one of strategic outcomes that you've agreed to support. When there are apparent important improvements that need to be made that don't link to one of these objectives, you may need to revisit them and identify what may have been overlooked in the initial planning. For example, someone might identify later that you need to improve the process for publishing data sets – maybe there should have been an additional outcome to, say, only release tested and approved data to the public.

Stick with the problems and avoid proposing solutions

The purpose of the workshop is to draw out and record the problems that need to be addressed by your future data management strategy. There is a risk that conversations morph into problem-solving discussions that aren't needed at this time - these will only bog down the workshop. These discussions should be parked and then addressed in later workshops designed to investigate solutions.

Use the DAMA wheel as a roadmap

An effective method for systematically identifying an organisation's data problems is to establish a helicopter view of the problems by working through each part of the DAMA wheel and addressing each component area in turn.

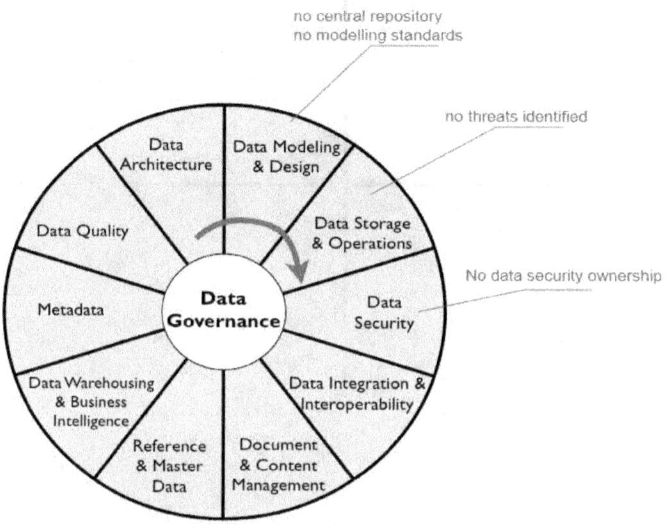

As you hopefully have the key data stakeholders in the room, it will be effective to step through each domain and ask the group, in general terms, what problems, if any, exist in each domain that are creating problems for teams. It is likely that for some domains there are no significant problems being experienced, and in other domains there may be only minor irritants. The key outcome must be to identify those domains with important and urgent problems that need to be addressed.

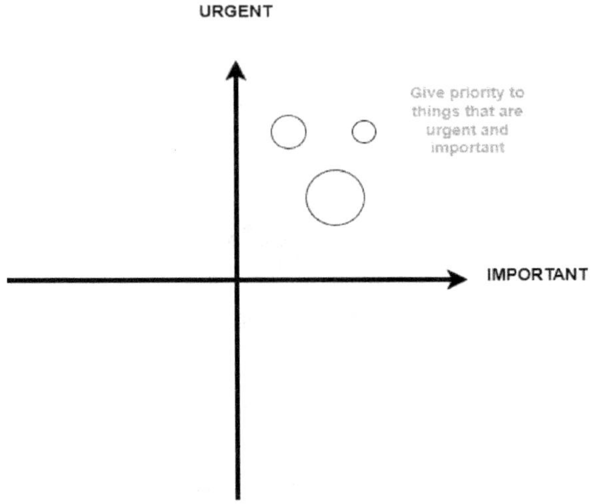

It is important to identify the business problems being experienced and a measure of the consequences being felt. Keep away from technical discussions as you are trying to keep everything understandable by non-technical people.

To identify how bad a particular issue may be, a t-shirt measure is a good approach. This quantifies magnitudes with values of Extra-Large, Large, Medium, and Small. Hopefully you don't have any 4XL problem areas!

Once you've been through each segment of the wheel and identified the business problem magnitudes, you then need to step back and decide which segments need priority. You should then apply a High/Medium/Low categorization to each segment to identify how urgently the problems need to be addressed. It is not practical to have more than one or two High priority segments because you really don't want to be battling on more than one or two fronts at the same time. Similar to the approach used for selecting the data Crown Jewels, you need to sift through all the problems being experienced and identify which ones are relatively more important than the others. While all problems may seem important, there will be some that cause more organisational pain than others or some that prohibit the organisation from achieving important strategic outcomes.

At the end of the process, you ideally have a wheel diagram annotated with the segments that need to be addressed within your planned timeframe.

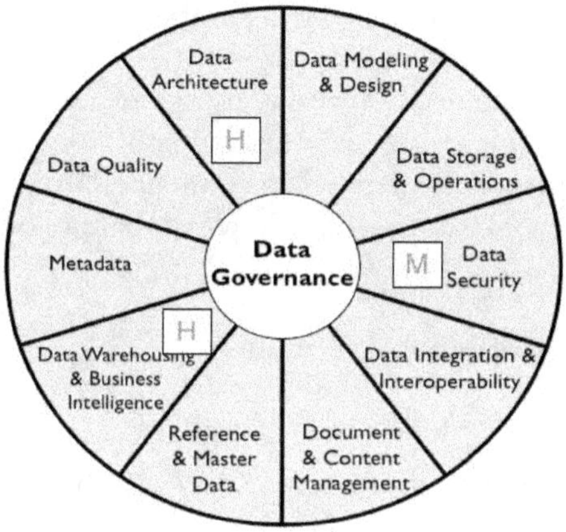

Documenting the workshop results

If the workshop has been completed successfully, you should have the following:

- a set of vision statements that identify the business improvements that you want data management to deliver or contribute to
- an annotated DAMA wheel that identifies the domains that have significant problems to be addressed
- a list of problems to be fixed or areas for improvement

Because these outcomes have been derived from the data stakeholders of your organisation, it is reasonable to consider that you have a good set of requirements to be addressed in your initial data management strategy. Remember that this isn't set in concrete and may need to be changed or added to later after some reflection.

Recap

With any system development, you need to have the requirements documented before you start building anything. In this case we are building a data management capability, so it also has requirements.

The proposed data management capability must address the needs of the organisation and not some theoretical requirements from a textbook or body of knowledge. If the needs are derived from the major data stakeholders, then you will have more support and less interference than if you try to identify and decide them yourself.

Running a data management problem workshop is a good way of:

- demonstrating leadership in data management
- building a relationship with the senior data stakeholders
- introducing the DAMA framework to the organisation and showing how it can be used to decompose the broad data management domain into a set of focused capabilities
- quickly identifying the key data problems facing the organisation and their relative priorities
- working with the stakeholders to establish a rough plan of attack for addressing the high priority problems
- gaining a shared vision for how data management needs to be managed in your organisation.

DEVELOPING A DATA MANAGEMENT STRATEGY

Keep your strategy focussed

Before you start this strategy, it's important to be clear about its purpose, and who is going to use it and why. It is easy to waste your time producing a document that goes nowhere and gets ignored – instead, we want to produce a document that is recognised as the approved roadmap of what you plan to do with data management. I'm sure many of you have seen fileserver folders full of documents that nobody ever looks at – and we don't want to produce one more of these.

So, who will or should use it?

- Your top-level information management committee should be able to clearly see the business outcomes that you plan to improve and over what timeframes. They will be able to see the extent of current operational problems created by a lack of proper data management.
- The CIO will be able to see the outcomes that the IT group are planning to deliver, and the magnitude of resources required. This will have a direct impact on IT resource planning and prioritization.
- The data stakeholders will see what data management changes are going to be made and how their teams will benefit. They should recognise that their concerns are being addressed.
- The data management team will see a prioritized work plan and see how their work will contribute to the overall organisation.

Avoid the TL;DR outcome

"TL;DR" is short for "too long – didn't read". It's important that a strategy document provides only enough information for its purpose and avoids becoming too large for people to be interested in reading.

Remember, you may be the only one in your organization that is actually excited about data management - to everyone else, it may be just a black box that should result in better quality and better managed data. In any strategy document you need to focus on explaining what you plan to do and selling the benefits to the organisation and the data stakeholders. Don't put them to sleep with detail!

The big-picture in the strategy

A data management strategy is a formal plan that identifies the activities, resources, and controls necessary to achieve a particular vision for the management of an organisation's data.

As opposed to your recognition strategy that is your own "internal marketing" plan, a data management strategy is one that needs to be published and accepted by senior management. It should be seen as comparable with any other strategic IT plan for the organisation, and it should tell the reader what you plan to do to improve the organisation's data management and the outcomes that you expect to deliver.

Ideally, the data management strategy should be delivering something that is already promised or required by an existing parent strategy. For example, if you already have some form of enterprise data strategy, then the data management strategy can be linked directly to outcomes and activities of this strategy. It will be a real benefit if you can be seen to be supporting an existing strategy rather than being seen as something independent of all the other IT-related strategies for the organisation.

If there's no existing enterprise data strategy, you may need to study any existing corporate strategic plan so that you can identify any objectives that will need some data management in order to deliver. For example, if there's a strategic plan that wants to deliver customer self-service 24x7, then they'll need to have data available, deployed, and accurate, 24x7.

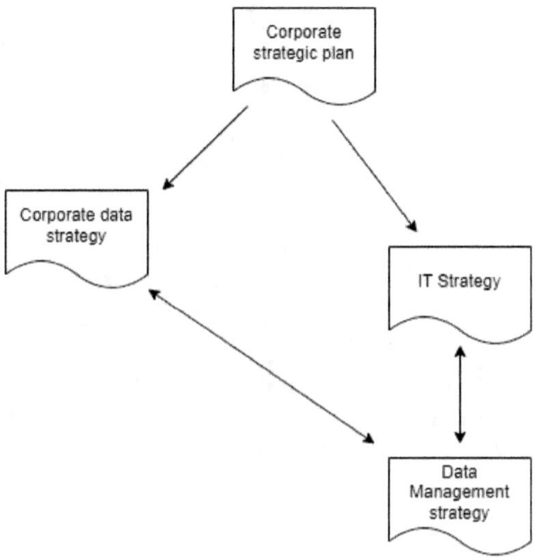

This diagram shows that while the Data Management strategy inherits requirements from both a Corporate Data Strategy and an IT Strategy, it also informs both with critical deficiencies and initiatives.

The following diagram shows a hypothetical scenario where there is an established corporate objective of reducing operational costs. This is supported by the IT Strategic Plan that identifies IT strategic objectives of reducing development costs and reducing system development times – both of which independently will result in reducing the overall operational costs. In this example, data management will support the reduction of IT development costs by automating database deployments, and this requires an activity involving selecting and implementing automated database deployment tools. In parallel to this, the data management team will be supporting the reduction in IT development times by reducing the time taken to design database changes, and this will be achieved by adopting agile database design processes.

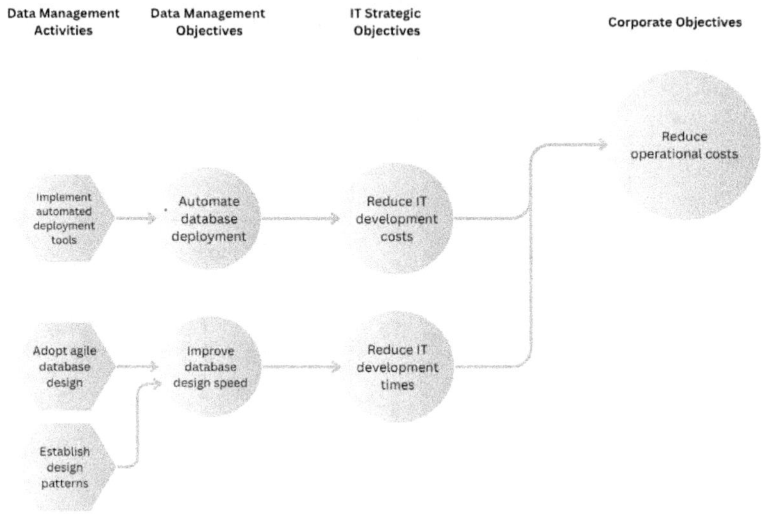

In this way, proposed data management activities can not only be linked directly to strategic IT initiatives, but also to key corporate objectives. Any executive reading your data management strategy can easily see your proposed activities, what you will be delivering, and how these contribute to the overall corporate objectives. The good thing here is that you are seen as supporting objectives that have already been approved.

Set the right timeframe for your strategy

You'll need to give some consideration about the timeframe that you expect your strategy to run. Being realistic, you probably can't even predict what the IT business will look like in 5 years, so maybe plan for a period less than this.

I find it useful to think in terms of "this is what we're doing now, and we're expecting to do this stuff later". The reality is that as IT resources and technology change in the future, you'll need to keep re-thinking the activities that you thought you'd be performing in the future. As the timeframe extends, you need to be increasingly vague about specifics and focus more on the better outcomes that will be delivered.

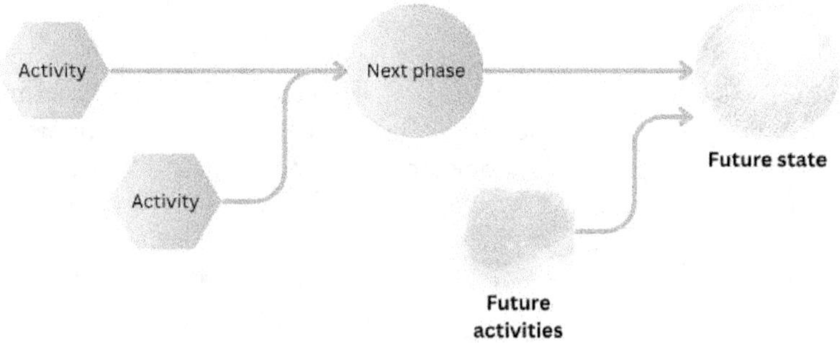

What should be in a data management strategy?

The data management strategy should be an easy-to-read roadmap of areas to be improved and the activities that need to be done to achieve these.

The contents of a data management strategy could be the subject of a book itself, and of course it depends on what needs to be done specifically for each organisation. So, while it's not possible to be definitive, it is possible to offer some suggestions.

Be guided by the DMBOK

Don't try to re-invent the wheel – make use of the existing DMBOK wheel instead. Leverage the industry-standard view of what constitutes proper "data management" and use the existing DMBOK framework to shape your strategy. Just as if you were going to improve your organisation's accounting processes - you would leverage the standard accounting practices and not try to define them yourself.

Look at each component of the DMBOK wheel and answer the questions:

- What is our target state?
- Where are we now?
- What problems are we experiencing?
- How can we get from the current to the target state?

Be clear about your direction

Make sure you know what an acceptable level of maturity is for your current timeframe. It is likely to be impractical to aim for a high level of maturity across the board, and you should perhaps aim to only increase maturity in one or two areas and maybe only by one step. Remember that it's better to under-promise and over-deliver.

Every activity that you plan to do or improve must move you towards one of your approved objectives. Avoid activities that seem like a popular or attractive idea that aren't really taking you in a direction that you want to go.

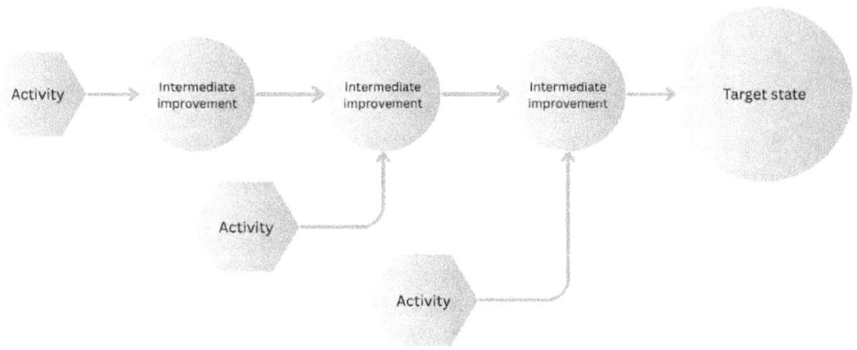

Prioritize your improvements

You are likely to have limited resources, so ensure that you focus on improvements that move you in the right directions, even if they are modest.

You may not be able to start working on critical weaknesses initially - you might have to start gaining practical experience by implementing something less critical instead of tackling something hard and then failing. Success with smaller stepping-stones may not only provide valuable lessons about how to get things done in your organisation, but it can help you start a track record as an achiever.

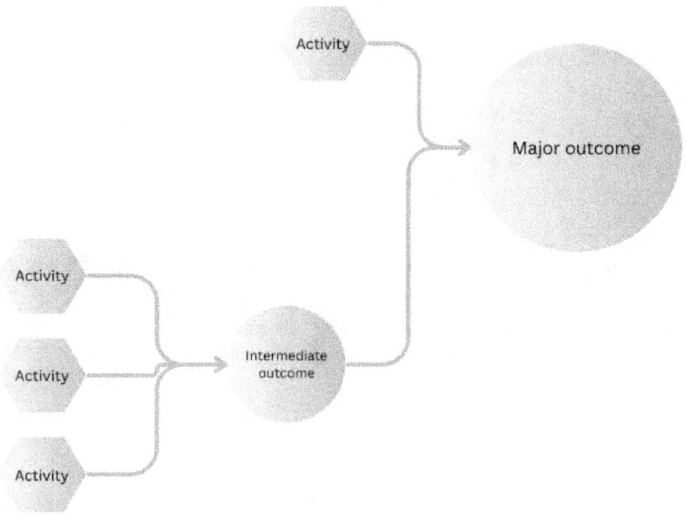

Be pragmatic – set achievable intermediate target milestones

If your organisation is immature in its data management, then delivering the desirable end-state is probably impossible to achieve quickly. Instead, identify one or more milestones that are achievable within an acceptable time frame. A good target for intermediate delivery is three to six months. Don't delude yourself and over-promise.

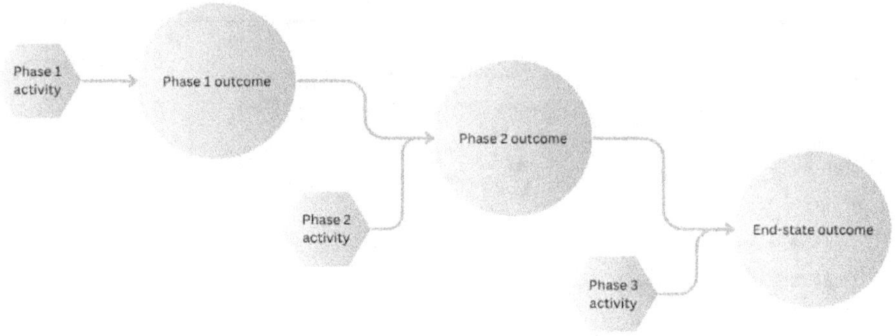

Good data management is about continual improvement, and as it involves people, processes, and technology, improvements are likely to take time to get right and become standard practice within your organisation.

Match data management outcomes with organisational outcomes

Always keep in mind that a lot of people don't understand data management as deeply as you, and just because you think something is important, don't make the mistake of thinking that others will automatically think the same.

You must be able to link data management objectives with an objective that other people in the organisation feel will be valuable. The following table provides some example equivalences.

Data management objective	**Equivalent organisation objective**
Clean up customer addresses	Reduce the cost of undeliverable mail
Establish a data asset register	Understand which data stores hold risky personal information that must be protected. Identify where we are holding multiple copies of the same data and increasing our storage costs.
Establish a data change coordination process	Ensure that corporate reporting teams have adequate warnings about upcoming changes.

To move forward with any of your initiatives you need to be able to communicate how they are going to benefit the organisation or other teams.

Ensure your strategy clearly delivers on organisational priorities

Your strategy needs to be attractive to senior management, so make sure that casual readers can easily see how you are supporting desirable organisation outcomes. Don't rely on lower-level details to sell your case. Don't assume that people will see an objective and automatically understand what benefits it delivers to them or the organisation. Make a clear path between problem and solution, because this might be as far as they read.

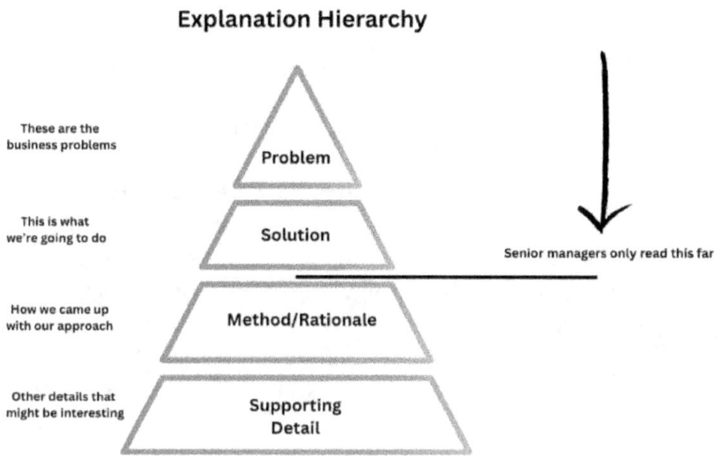

If your organisation has a corporate strategic plan, then each of your planned activities and outcomes needs to be linked directly to something within that plan. If you are proposing an initiative that isn't contributing to an endorsed strategic outcome, then people will question why you're doing it and why they should support it. Never forget that you are competing with other teams for resources and funding, so you need to create recognition that if these data management activities aren't performed then the high-level corporate objectives may not be met.

Review your data management strategy from the perspective of various people in the Executive – will it convince the Director of Finance to make funds available? Will it convince the COO that operational costs will be reduced by removing damaging IT coordination problems?

Where to start your data management strategy?

This is a major decision point in your overall data management journey. Hopefully it can bring together both the work you've done on your private recognition plan and your public data management strategizing.

Remember, the data management strategy will be the corporately-approved path for the short- and medium-term, and it needs to be recognised and agreed to by your peers as a strategy that should be followed and supported. As a result, it can't be seen as something that you've come up with yourself – even if the final outcome is exactly what you wanted in the first place.

As part of your recognition strategy, you will have identified the key stakeholders or influencers in data and data management within your organisation. This group of people that must conclude: "This strategy is going to be beneficial for me". Anyone who doesn't think this way may become a blocker downstream. It is important that this group of people have an investment in your strategy; ideally, it reflects all the improvements that they would collectively like, and that there's something in it for everyone.

Turn your annotated DAMA wheel into something concrete

A good way to start your data management strategy is to turn the results of the previous requirements-gathering workshop into a plan for delivery. This will allow you to build on a foundation that is already understood by the key data stakeholders, so there's no need to try and establish a new framework. It is also a benefit if others see that you've taken the workshop outcomes and elaborated them further, and they'll need less explanation of what you're trying to achieve.

With this approach, you need to develop a sub-strategy for each segment of the DAMA wheel, with each sub-strategy clearly stating any agreed data management problems within the segment and how you plan to fix them.

The following diagram shows that following your examination of each segment you can create a sub-strategy that explains what objectives are planned for that segment and what initiatives will be undertaken and over what timeframe.

This approach will result in easily digestible sub-strategies focused on specific data management segments. For example, you may have sub-strategy discussing data architecture deficiencies and plans for addressing them, or a master-data sub-strategy focused particularly on your master data problems. This will help ensure that your data management strategy is focused on actual objectives and activities and will be more meaningful to the stakeholders.

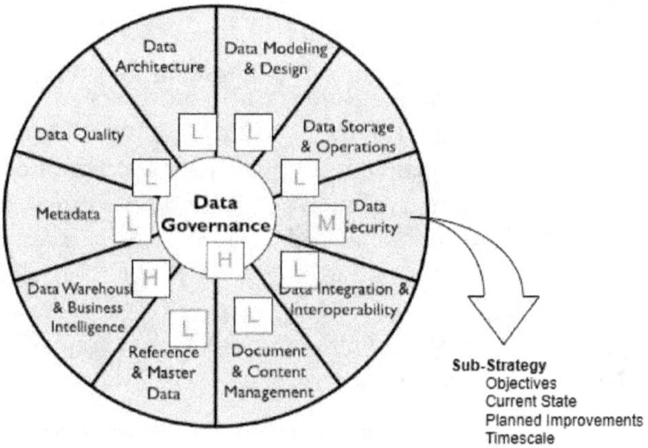

Be more specific in the short-term and more vague for later objectives

As with any agile development, you need to be quite specific about what you plan to address and to deliver in the short term but allow for priorities and problems to change as time progresses.

In reality, none of us really knows what the IT landscape will look like in five years, so avoid trying to predict it. However, you can't ignore it either, so you just need to lay out a plan of attack for what you *think* you'll be working on, with an understanding that it's a living document that you'll keep updated as things change.

> If we use a hiking analogy here, people would be comfortable with you being clear about how you are going to climb a ridge just in front of you and, once you reach the top, reassessing specifically how you'll get down the other side.

Educate as well as explain your strategy

You can't always predict who is going to read your strategy, so you shouldn't rely on a reader having the same background knowledge as you.

As a result, the strategy needs to educate the audience about the future vision, the current problems and the resulting current and/or future consequences of these problems, and how you plan to overcome these problems. Don't assume that the reader knows <u>anything</u> about data or data management.

Say what you're going to do and then do what you say

One of the important lessons that I've learnt from years of IT projects and audits is that you need to be clear about what you plan to do and make sure that you actually do it. You can lose all professional credibility if you say that you're going to do something and then go off and do something else. Nobody may ever believe you again and auditors usually watch for non-compliances like this.

Don't be over-ambitious and promise something that you won't deliver just to make your plan more impressive. Be realistic about what you can achieve.

Find the low-hanging fruit

With any strategy that needs stakeholder support, you need to provide some tangible benefits or wins so that you get permitted to continue. You don't want to be in a position where after six or twelve months you haven't actually delivered any benefit. IT development strategies such as Agile have reinforced the concept of delivering early (and fixing later), so there may be a broad expectation that you'll deliver something quickly.

If you can, make sure that some visible quick wins are delivered in each phase of the strategy.

Be punchy

This strategy is likely to be the first formal document that you or your data management team has produced for the Executive and key data stakeholders, so it needs to have impact.

In this case, "impact" means:

- It is easy to consume (remember the TL;DR warning)
- The data management problems in the organisation are clear, and the consequences of these problems are readily understandable from the perspective of a business user, not an IT specialist
- The plan for addressing the problems is clear and logical
- You've clearly justified which problems are given priority and why.

Don't assume that the reader has been in the requirements gathering workshop, so make sure that the document can stand alone. A good strategy is to pick a senior executive as a virtual target and ensure that if this person were to read the document, they would understand what you plan to do and why, and also the consequences of doing nothing.

Before you start, set yourself some targets such as these.

- The overall strategy will be no more than 6-10 pages long
- If there is some essential information that must be included to support the strategy, then move it to an appendix so it doesn't interrupt the strategy flow
- Each problem that is addressed by the strategy will be supported by a diagram that guides the reader directly from problem to ultimate solution.

Sub-strategy detail

We said earlier that the overall strategy can be broken down into a set of sub-strategies, each of which is focused on a single segment of the DAMA wheel.

Each sub-strategy needs to be self-sufficient and tell the reader what your plans are for that segment. It will be up to you to decide how much detail you need to include and whether each sub-strategy needs supporting detail or not. However, each sub-strategy is likely to at least need the following addressed:

- The broad vision of what the segment contributes to your organisation. This is important because most people, even those in IT, won't have any understanding of the segments outside their direct involvement. For example, your organisation may have multiple document repositories, with each used for different purposes. Similarly, you may have important customer data stored across multiple application databases.
- The current deficiencies in the segment (if any) that will be addressed by the strategy. This needs to be a combination of specific problems that need to be addressed and the business consequences of the problem. For example, inaccurate customer address data may lead to mail being returned with a consequential cost to the organisation as well as interruptions and delays to business processes that result in KPI impacts.

- Proposed initiatives to remediate either the problem or its consequences. Remember that initiatives can be delivered in multiple parts spread across multiple phases.
- The likely timeframes for delivering initiatives and, just as importantly, when these will be delivering a benefit to the organisation.

You might want to consider avoiding any implementation details in this document as you are laying out a set of problems and a strategy for addressing them. Maybe consider suggesting that the strategy will be followed by an implementation plan that provides further detail.

Recap

You need to develop a data management strategy that:

- is easily consumed by people who are not knowledgeable about data management,
- educates the reader about the scope of data management in your organisation,
- explains the current data management problems and the consequences to the business,
- educates the reader on how you are addressing the reported data management problems by using the industry standard DAMA framework,
- outlines the activities that you plan to undertake to mitigate the problems and the proposed timing and dependencies of these activities,
- identifies the outcomes you will be delivering, and
- provides a future vision for data management and the potential benefits to the organisation.

You want the people reading your strategy to recognise that this document is laying out a structured roadmap for addressing important data-related issues that, if not fixed, will cause extensive down-stream problems in the future.

BEING PRAGMATIC ABOUT YOUR DEVELOPMENT ARTIFACTS

When is this chapter relevant?

This chapter becomes relevant whenever you want to plan any data management activities. This could be early-on, perhaps when you're developing your data management strategy, or it could be later when you are just developing a plan for the next several months.

Why do I need to focus on artifacts?

Deciding on the artifacts you'll develop is important because they become the tangible products that you can distribute to other teams or managers and reference when promoting your achievements. Without tangible artifacts, it can be difficult to demonstrate value to others.

The artifacts don't need to be large or complex volumes to meet your objectives – they just need to be appropriate for their given purpose. For example, if you have investigated the source of a data error you might produce a simple document that outlines the problem, its consequences, and a way forward that is easily digestible by the decision-makers that you want to submit it to. If you are running a coordination meeting, you'd likely want to produce some form of minutes that document decisions made at those meetings, or action items that were agreed.

This chapter will help you decide what data management artifacts you need to produce and how much work you need to put into each of them. This is important because you don't want to waste your time developing documents that no-one wants or cares about. When you do identify important artifacts to be developed you also don't want to over-engineer them or make them longer or more complex than they need to be.

Unfortunately, data management artifacts aren't something that can usually be found in textbooks or the DMBOK because it depends on your organisation, industry, technology, and problems that need solving.

All we can reasonably do is review industry-standard guidelines to help us make sensible decisions.

General guidelines

Be pragmatic

Pragmatism suggests we should only develop artifacts that are actually useful to the people in the trenches. Over my career I have often seen documents on bookshelves that haven't been looked at for years and I wonder about the amount of effort that went into producing something that is essentially ignored. I'm sure you don't want your work to go the same way.

Before you start any artifact, think to yourself – and maybe put the answer on its front page – "who will be using this document and for what purpose?". If this isn't clear, then don't bother starting the document.

Don't aim for perfection

Being pragmatic means recognizing that there's a continuum that stretches from "we've got nothing" all the way up to "we have an encyclopedia on the subject". As soon as you've reached the first rung up the ladder that is above "we've got nothing", then you've added some value. From there, you just need to decide how far up the ladder you need to climb before you can switch focus to somewhere else that needs attention.

Never aim for perfection – it's something that you'll never get close to anyway – it's more likely that before you even get close some technology will change and pull the rug from under your feet and you'll have to rethink what you've already developed.

Aim instead for "good enough for now". And, as shown in the following diagram, it's likely that your maturity will differ wildly across the various data management components. Some areas may be delivering acceptable value while being quite immature compared to ideal solutions.

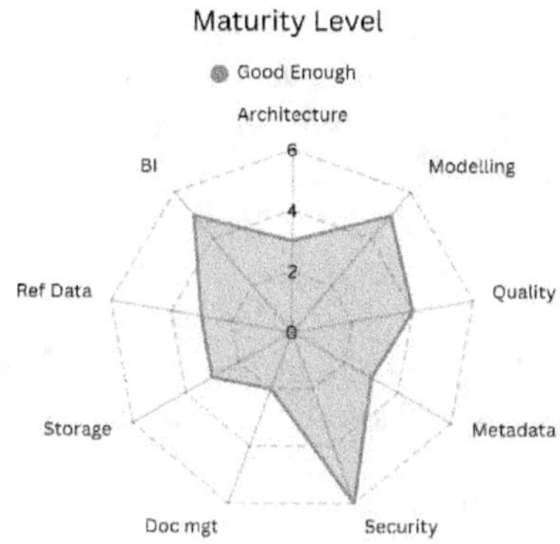

Avoid the concept of a "final" version

This really follows from the previous point. Stay away from versioning schemes like "Draft" and "Final". I've been in many organisations where we actively used "Draft v25.0" because making something "Final" implied it was finished and we were always finding new improvements.

Instead, I recommend a versioning system that keeps it simple, such as the following:

- v0.n (eg v0.8) – draft, useful for shaping ideas and narrative, but not ready for people to use yet
- v1.0 – the first version of the document that is "good enough" for people to actually use. This one has probably incorporated feedback from others.
- VN.0 – just another iteration of the document, recognizing that more might come in the future.
- vN.n (eg v25.1) – when you need to convey that this is maybe a minor improvement to v25 and that v25 itself may still be ok for people to use.

Avoid producing dead documents and stay agile

A dead document is one that, after development, usually sits on a shelf and is ignored. Sometimes this is called *shelfware*, and there is nothing more depressing if you were its author.

Our goal is to avoid producing dead documents and instead produce artifacts that people want to use and maintain. People will only bother maintaining something if it provides benefit to them, so this must be the objective of any data management deliverable. As I've said earlier, before you produce anything you need to ask yourself, "who will use this and why?". If you can't answer this, then you're well on the path of creating a dead document. You should also consider putting this information in the document's introduction so that the reader knows that you've tried to produce a live document, not a dead one. If there are particular circumstances when the document needs to be reviewed, then record this as well so that people know when they themselves may have to update it. These circumstances might just be a suggested future review date, or some other event such as the replacement of a dependent technology.

Sometimes documents encourage their own death because of inappropriate record management. If everything you produce needs to be a Word document that has two approval signatures and stored in a document management system, then the overhead of updating it, getting it re-approved, and re-issuing it dissuades people from the effort of updating it. I've experienced this many times – you see an error or omission in a document and then realise it's too much effort to update and re-issue.

Consider more lightweight forms of documentation such as modern online collaboration tools that allow people to easily flag things that are wrong or even to just update the documentation whenever they see something that needs to be corrected or extended.

Whenever you can, stay out of the forever war with the compliance folks who believe that everything official should be a document in a document management system. Unless documents are easily found by a casual browser, then you may just be building an elephants graveyard[4] of artifacts.

It's hard enough sometimes to get people to read the documentation, so don't make it even harder!

What type of artifacts might you need to produce?

Typically, good data management governance requires that we produce tangible artifacts that can be used, reviewed, corrected, and improved over time. It's hard to improve something that's not actually defined in the first place.

Possible documents/artifacts

Perhaps the best way to identify possible data management artifacts is to step our way around the DAMA wheel and look at each domain separately.

Data governance

This is all about processes, standards, and controls, so you'll likely need to produce:

- policies
- procedures
- standards
- guidelines (we like these a lot because they can provide guidance and standardization without being a mandatory straight-jacket)

---

[4] https://en.wiktionary.org/. A place where, according to legend, older elephants instinctively direct themselves when they reach a certain age, in order to die alone. (by extension) A place where lost objects or people end up, and from which there is no escape.

- roles and responsibilities
- metrics

Data architecture

- architecture diagrams (there are thousands to choose from!)
- architecture models using professional modelling tools
- architecture standards and principles that explain "how we do things around here". These documents capture the data rules and decisions that have already been made that developers need to follow.
- Data catalogs

Data development and design

- data models
- data modelling rules, policies, and conventions for how models should be developed for the organisation so that there is consistency across projects.

Data operations

- Policies, procedures, and conventions for how data is managed operationally by the organisation. Eg how important data is replicated and protected and how data storage is optimised for access.
- SLAs for data stores, eg which ones are 24x7 and which are office hours only
- Access controls over data access
- Audit requirements over data changes

Master data management & reference data

- Registers of master data and reference data repositories
- Processes and responsibilities for maintaining master data repositories
- Processes for validating repositories

Data quality

- Data quality rules that allow objective measurements of quality and deviations from approved rules
- data quality analyses and reports

Interoperability

- Data migration and transformation rules
- Data replication details

Document management

- Document repository registers
- document management rules, eg retention, culling and archiving rules

Business Intelligence

- warehouse DB schema designs including data transformation logic
- reporting schema designs
- other schema designs used for enterprise reporting

Metadata management

- Architecture diagrams showing metadata repositories and metadata access and publishing tools
- Documentation of metadata that is published externally

There is no prescriptive list to rely on!

Unfortunately, there's no definitive list of data management artifacts that need to exist for a well-running practice. In fact, the existence of something like this could be a real problem by misleading teams into thinking that the creation of all the documents is what you need to focus on. In reality, implementing a good data management practice involves working out what problems need to be solved, what artifacts will help your stakeholders, and taking everyone on the journey of deciding what should be in them and making sure that everyone gains value from them.

There is no advantage to being seen spending your time producing documentation that others consider a waste of time. This may or may not be true, but what others think is important if you want them to support you.

You need to think for yourself

Following on from the previous paragraphs, there is no substitute for working out your essential set of artifacts.

> Early in my career my world was defined by DOD-STD-1679 and then DOD-STD-2167. These were military standards that outlined the requirements for building software for everything from a missile control system to a battleship. They defined everything you needed to design and document to meet the software development quality standards. They were big documents and, along with their family of related specifications, they defined the whole software development and testing process.
>
> I often saw developers blindly taking a template and religiously writing something under every heading. Even if they were only producing a system to manage vehicle bookings, they'd probably still populate the sections on how to minimize the accidental release of a nuclear weapon.
>
> I'd get one of these documents to review and sometimes they were so complicated that I'd end up confused about what the system was required to do, or why there was a risk of a vehicle dropping a nuke in the carpark. But I did understand why the person took so long to produce a useless document.

If you blindly follow someone else's roadmap, then you'll likely miss the essential step of working out what your problems actually need. And you'll probably waste a lot of time and effort doing so.

> Later, they issued a new standard that provided guidance on how to customize DOD-STD-2167. It had useful suggestions that were the equivalent of "take the template and delete every heading that isn't relevant for your project", and "only design components necessary for your solution".

DMBOK can also suggest a lot of possible deliverables, so you need to be wary of this.

Getting the balance right

Having gone through the process and deciding what artifacts you are going to produce, you then must make a strategic decision about how to make the artifacts readily accessible to the people that you expect will need them.

Oh, no – there's another risk here. Are you going to produce a huge impenetrable tome containing all the data management policies, or a raft of 20 separate policy documents that people must wade through?

Having made the wrong decision a few times in the past, I can provide the following recommendations:

- Documents are harder to maintain and publish than web pages in a collaboration environment.
- Documents are often necessary if policies need to be officially version-controlled and approved. For example, a policy for emergency Production database changes may need to have visible authenticity such as the CEO's signature on the front.
- Small documents or pages that focus on a narrow subject are easier to consume and are more likely to be read.
- When there are multiple documents involved, it can be useful to have a graphical document tree showing their relationships. For example, a diagram can easily show that a parent Data Management Plan has subordinate Data Quality, Metadata Management, and Data Design Plans.

Nothing here is particularly complex to solve, but it is something you want to think about before deciding what you are going to produce.

The importance of discussion papers

So, what is a discussion paper?

Discussion papers are a great way of presenting an idea in a non-threatening way. Using the term "discussion paper" tells people that you are putting it out there for discussion and feedback, but importantly, you're not issuing it as something as potentially troublesome as a new draft policy.

Discussion papers can be good way to just organise some ideas and communicate them in a focused way to a group of stakeholders.

The modern way of working is that people are often unlikely to read your policies, procedures, and standards, or fully understand the implications for the work that is currently in front of them. A discussion paper is a way of collecting and organizing ideas, an approach, a proposal, or a way of doing business, and shaping this into a (hopefully) easy to consume document that is easy to read and actually helpful.

A collection of discussion papers might end up being like a set of FAQs that makes it easier for people to find "how it's done around here".

> As an example, maybe your organisation has evolved a standard approach for managing data replication using different tools and techniques for different types of problem. You could create a discussion paper on, say, "Data replication for operational systems" where you outline what tools should be used for which purpose, what rules or standards apply, and importantly, you can provide the rationale of why this approach has been adopted. If possible, you might be able to link to parent policies and standards, but this is probably irrelevant to someone who just wants to design a data replica for some new application.

The whole purpose of the discussion paper is to provide clarity to the designer about the decisions that need to be made and the criteria that need to be considered.

Discussion papers don't need to live in any systematic framework

Discussion papers are things that I have found invaluable over my career. They are often overlooked in organisations because they don't seem to have a natural place in formal governance.

This is, in fact, their strength. You just develop discussion papers as the need arises to explain some part of your data management solution.

You can reference them whenever and wherever it makes sense.

Discussion papers are "unofficial"

As discussion papers aren't policies, procedures, or standards, they are more unofficial. You may use one to document some aspect of how things are done, and sometimes you'll need tacit approval from others and at other times you'll just use them yourself to explain how things work. The reality is that sometimes you'll write a paper that starts a discussion and eventually you'll realise it's wrong or deficient, and you'll discard it.

Keeping them officially "unofficial" allows you to be agile.

Discussion papers may only be a brain dump

In data architecture we'll establish ways of doing things that meet all our requirements, sometimes after multiple iterations and dead ends, but the hard-won lessons have ended up as tacit knowledge that's only in people's heads.

Discussion papers can be a great way of capturing the whole problem/design/rationale logic so that others can understand the hows and whys. They can be efficient subject-specific brain-dumps.

Discussion papers may not gain any formal agreement

As mentioned earlier, discussion papers may or may not get reviewed and formally approved. But this doesn't mean there isn't agreement that what they capture is correct.

As a data manager it will be your job to publish both the ones that are agreed and the ones that are merely brain dumps. The key objective is to get the ideas visible to the people who design and build systems.

Recap on discussion papers

- Issue-specific papers that can, for example, explain design patterns and the rationale behind each pattern.
- They may just contain a brain-dump of some data management implementation that needs to be captured for the benefit of later developers.
- Usually, they don't need formal approval processes.
- Usually, they don't need to be part of any formal documentation tree.
- Collecting them and making them public and accessible is very important

Recap

This chapter provided some guidelines about how to be pragmatic about your selection of data management artifacts that you decide to produce.

There are some significant risks that you need to avoid:

- The risk that you'll produce artifacts that no-one values
- The risk that you'll over-engineer an artifact and make it more comprehensive than is really required for the problem that you are trying to solve initially, leading to wasted time and effort
- The risk that you'll try to produce something perfect instead of "good enough"
- The risk that others can't easily navigate or consume the artifacts

The chapter provided some recommendations to help you avoid the risks by:

- ensuring that you know who will use an artifact and for what purpose before spending time developing it
- accepting that documents have a lifecycle that never becomes "final"
- avoiding an overly official update or release process that stifles making small corrections and improvements
- avoiding the creation of dead documents and shelfware
- make documentation easily consumable and organized so that people can easily see what is available and pick only what they want to read

Finally, the chapter discusses the benefits of creating discussion papers as an efficient way of recording how and why some things are done in your organisation. Also using them as a tool for capturing ideas from others that you can reflect back to them for agreement.

BEING PRAGMATIC IN HOW YOU WORK

Why this is important

You are likely to have limited time and resources available to implement data management processes. The previous chapter showed that you need to carefully consider the documents or other artifacts that you produce so that they deliver real business value. Similarly, you must plan where you are going to target your efforts so that they address real business problems for your organization. You also need to consider how much effort to apply to a given problem so that you don't get bogged down delivering ever-diminishing returns. You want the best "bang for the buck" you can get.

The risk of trying too hard

There can be a tendency to read your DMBOK and identify a lot of things that your organisation needs to do and document. Approaching the problem from this perspective can be risky because you can end up spending a lot of time on things that the organisation doesn't care about and may not support. Instead, you need to focus on the urgent and important problems that need addressing. The less urgent and less important improvements can be made another day, and you will avoid building a huge backlog of planned improvements that you'll need to publish, maintain, explain, and likely never deliver.

This is where pragmatism comes into play.

Being pragmatic

Whenever you identify a missing piece of data management, you need to ask yourself three questions:

- What happens if I do nothing now and worry about it later?

- How much planning and documentation is "good enough" to head off current problems?
- How much time and resources do I have available to work on this?

What is mandatory and what is merely desirable? Let's look at an example.

> Let's say you have one or more systems that collect data, pass this data to a central system-of-record, which then distributes sets of data to several reporting and/or analysis systems. Some data is also extracted and made available for external data consumers. After investigation, you realise there's no useful metadata available describing the transport, storage, or transformation of this data.

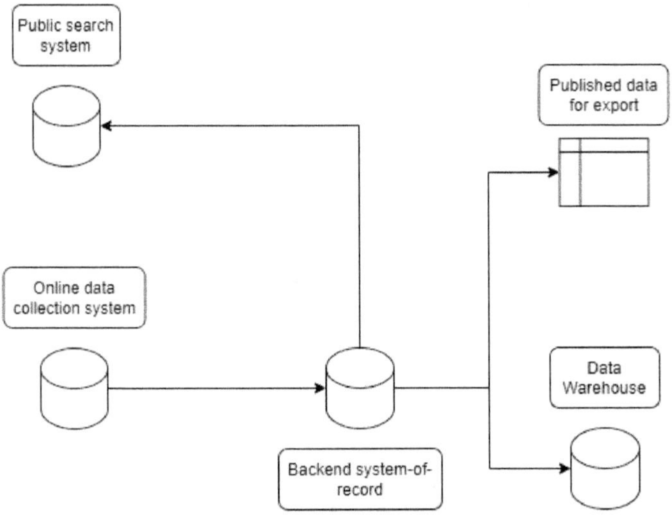

If you wanted to start capturing and recording the metadata describing this data pipeline, where would you start? From a metadata management perspective, there are many items that need documenting, from database designs, data flows, ETL transformations, data warehouse aggregations and derivations, etc.

A purist would say that the full data pipeline needs to be documented, from the databases in the data collection systems through the various transformations until the data is stored in the analysis/reporting databases. This would likely take a lot of time and effort, maybe several years if you were to do it all. However, if we apply a pragmatic lens, we'd probably consider that the most critical components that must be documented would be:

- the data definitions in the system-of-record, and
- the data definitions that should be supplied alongside the published data files

Why just these components?

It's obviously a risk management call based on experience, but the rationale would be something like this:

- The data collection systems are systems-of-entry, and the data stores are likely optimized to suit the application rather than a master data repository. They may only hold transient data that is irrelevant once this data is passed to the backend system-of-record. The design of the data stores may also be less stable because agile application development may be making regular improvements. It is unlikely that any corporate BI reporting will be based on a data-entry system.
- Each data collection system may differ in its underlying data structure, and this means that different data transformations take place before the data is recorded in the system-of-record persistent data store.
- By definition, a system-of-record will be holding important enterprise data, and this master repository may end up distributing data to multiple other data repositories that act as a source of data for operational applications. It is likely that these distributed repositories will hold data in a format that is optimized for its parent application, and so each of these repositories is likely to hold different sets of data in possibly different formats.

- When data is published to external consumers you always need to provide supporting metadata. If the definitions that you provide are not accurate then there will likely be negative consequences, including reputational damage. These data definitions must be as correct as possible to avoid misleading your data consumers. Once data is outside your control it can be difficult to know who is using it and then explain problems or inadequacies.

> I once saw a situation where the definition of an exported field changed without the consumer being warned. A change to the definition of household income meant that business intelligence reports showed a substantial improvement in the national household income during the previous year, which was not correct. We were fortunate to understand our data well enough to see that a problem had arisen and we were able to identify that the metadata descriptions provided had not been updated and head off the problem before any reports became public. We learnt a valuable lesson about keeping published metadata accurate.

Don't be a control freak by staying in the past

I've been in this business a long time, and modern database developers would probably be horrified to learn about some of the standard data management practices that we followed decades ago.

> When you wanted to change a field/column definition you had to document all the required changes on a paper form, sign it, and take it to the data administration team. An administrative person would compare your signature with a specimen signature that they had on a card file, and if the two matched then they'd stamp and sign the form to validate your signature so that you could submit the change to the next change control board meeting. Even minor Production changes could take 3 months.

Over time, a lot of the practices that we thought were important have turned out not to be all that beneficial once technology improved.

> A common governance rule was having rigid naming standards for tables and columns, and many organisations insisted on constructing names from a set of approved abbreviations. You couldn't create a column called *person_first_name*, but had to use something like *prsn_nm_frst*. If a word didn't have an abbreviation in the official list, then a "new abbreviation" process was initiated to create one before your new column could be considered. The new abbreviation had to be published in the official abbreviation list before you were allowed to use it. Sometimes we spent a disproportionate amount of time just defining abbreviations for words rather than getting on with database designs.

Years ago, I stopped caring about official abbreviations and started worrying more about whether the column name was meaningful. If it made sense, then you could have it. This doesn't mean we didn't have any standards, but just because something was done in the past didn't mean that we had to treat it as gospel forever.

More generally, don't get caught up becoming a control freak who wants everything systematic. Everyone wants things agile these days, so only standardise things that are REALLY important.

Recap

This chapter focused on how to be pragmatic about:

- what data management activities you plan to do
- how much effort you put into each activity or artifact you plan on doing

There is a real trap in spending time trying to produce the best documents, procedures, standards, etc, when in reality there can be a diminishing benefit to additional work. You may find the 80/20 rule applies – the initial 20% effort will deliver 80% of the required benefit.

If you're starting from a position of low data management maturity, just getting some rudimentary processes or standards in operation may be good enough for you to focus on another area that urgently needs development. Consider the DMBOK as a set of recipes that you may selectively choose from and not something that needs to be followed religiously.

When you find an area that is seriously under managed, you should try and identify what are the most important components that need improvement and start with those and not automatically assume that all data management deficiencies are equally important. Consider using the Urgent/Important technique for deciding where you should focus initially.

Try to avoid being overly prescriptive and becoming seen as a barrier to rapid development. Identify the important rules that need to be followed and be flexible with others. This will assist you in being seen as supporting other teams and becoming a blocker – this is very important if your organisation is following Agile principles.

BRINGING IT ALL TOGETHER

The need for data management

Hopefully this book has helped you understand the business context of data management as it exists in a landscape of both IT and a wider organisation.

The need for data management isn't obvious to most people, including other IT professionals, so if you want to establish or extend a data management capability you need to invest time and effort in educating both your IT colleagues and upper management. You will only gain the support of others when they realise that good data management practices will help not only the organisation, but their own jobs as well. They need to understand that organisations without good data management are at a much higher risk of data loss, privacy violations, and reputational damage.

It's not possible for someone external to predict all the business drivers and blockers for data management in your organisation, but we've covered the more common ones. Reviewing these should have made you consider your own organisation to the point that now you can probably see better the levers that will motivate your own colleagues.

Make use of the DMBOK

The DAMA data management body of knowledge is an invaluable asset in making your colleagues view data management as a distinct and established discipline within IT.

Use this document whenever you can to reinforce the concept that your proposals and suggestions aren't just your personal opinions but are considered part of good professional practice that any organisation should have.

There is real recognition and authority to be gained by having an established Body of Knowledge and it means that you can refer to principles that it espouses without the need to justify them yourself.

Make sure the DMBOK is visible on your desk and maybe carry it around occasionally! Maybe drop it on desks from time to time so people appreciate how extensive it is by the "thunk" sound as it lands. Consultants understand the value of this "thunk factor" in boosting the credibility of their documents.

Plan your approach to data management

Regardless of how enthusiastic you are yourself; you want to establish a data management capability that becomes second-nature to your organisation and is not dependent on you personally to keep it alive.

Establishing a self-sustaining data management practice needs planning and careful implementation. It won't happen by accident.

There are two plans that need to be developed.

The first is a plan for how you will identify and build a relationship with key data stakeholders within your organisation. You will also need to gain an understanding of the data issues within the organisation and the consequences of these issues. You'll need this information to guide subsequent discussions and workshops, and it will help you to start creating a mental framework for how you could help these stakeholders in the future by creating the right processes and activities.

The second plan to be developed is the formal data management plan that identifies what data management capabilities you plan to deliver in the short- to medium-term and the benefits that will be delivered by these capabilities, including any problems fixed.

Key to the development of this second plan is a process that ensures you capture the key data stakeholders and carry them with you as you come up with a strategy. There will be one or more workshops required that need to flush out the organisation's data problems and their consequences. These workshops ensure that the stakeholders become aware of not only their own problems, but also the problems being experienced by the other stakeholders. You need the stakeholders to see the big-picture of your current data management environment including all the problems so that they can agree on which problems are more pressing for the organisation and which problems can be addressed later.

Your organisation's formal data management strategy will lay out the improvements in the organisation's data management environment that will be made in the short- to medium-term. The data stakeholders will see that this has evolved from their involvement, and they'll understand the rationale underpinning pragmatic decisions. There will be no need to re-justify the areas for improvement or explain the consequences to the organisation if the important and urgent problems aren't fixed.

This plan will become your roadmap for the future.

Understand your crown jewels

Your organisation will likely have a lot of data in the form of files, databases, datasets, and documents. The loss of some data could lead to the total collapse of the organisation, while the loss of other data might only be an inconvenience. The data management challenge is to identify the former from the latter. We can label this data as the organisation's *crown jewels*.

Identifying the crown jewels is a business process, and it needs the top executives of the organisation to be involved in the selection. In an environment where all data is deemed important it's not always an easy process to select the crown jewel data from the important or even critical data.

The main reason for identifying the crown jewel data is to allow you to prioritize the data and to ensure that you address the safety and integrity of this data before you consider the lesser data.

From the perspective of establishing data management in your organisation, identifying the crown jewel data has several benefits. Firstly, it forces engagement with the Executive as only they can truly nominate the relevant data. This engagement between the Executive and data management teams can be carried forward with other initiatives with the aim of keeping data management within the visibility of the executives. Secondly, identifying the crown jewel data gives the data management team a place to start developing any necessary governance controls, standards, and procedures.

An example of building upon the crown jewels could be the identification of data risks. Following the endorsement of the crown jewel data, the data management team can follow up with a discussion with the Executive about what risks the crown jewel data should be protected from.

Start with the Important and Urgent

Most organisations will potentially have lots of data management deficiencies that need to be addressed. However, we need to be pragmatic and consider:

- what data management resources are actually available
- when do you need to start delivering some benefits to the stakeholders
- from the list of all problems, what are the urgent and important ones that need to be given priority
- what quick wins are available even though they may not be both urgent and important

Being pragmatic

With the assumption that resources and budget are both limited, we must be pragmatic about what data management practices we implement. While the DMBOK is a comprehensive document, there's likely a need to satisfy some important business pressures:

- deliver some quick wins to demonstrate that you're delivering benefits
- delivering a mature data management capability may take a decade and you need to begin improving IT development much earlier

- technology is always changing, so you need to be flexible with what is implemented
- different problems can result in wildly different consequences with some far more important than others.

We need to develop a data management strategy that understands the relative importance of different datasets, the different business consequences of the range of data risks that exist, and the resources available to the data management team. As a result, we need to apply pragmatic prioritization rules to both the artifacts we produce and the deficiencies that we address.

A key pragmatic concept is the concept of "good enough". Aiming for perfection is a luxury that we will never have, and our key deliverable is something that is good enough to reduce risks to an acceptable level. Once we have achieved this, we can move on to addressing the problem with the next highest priority. We can always revisit solutions later and progressively improve them.

Final thoughts

Hopefully this book has shown you that the biggest data management challenge is the modern business environment, not just its IT environment.

The problems we've addressed so far have been related to:

- a broad corporate lack of understanding of data management and what it entails
- the need to compete with other corporate initiatives for resources
- gaining support from your organisation's Executive team in particular, as well as other data stakeholders
- planning the establishment of your data management practice so that it can be seen to deliver benefits to the whole organisation within acceptable timeframes and resource limits.

Before we can start work on improvements, we need to identify and address any blockers, because we can't improve the environment while there are factors that may be actively resisting our work.

We need to understand that before we make any improvements to data management capability, we need to understand the existing data problems and their consequences for the organisation overall as well as to other teams. All initiatives we propose need to be put in terms of business risks and benefits because we can't assume that key decision-makers and supporters have any technical knowledge of data management.

Finally, building a successful data management practice isn't about developing and imposing an efficient governance regime over an organisation's data, but rather, building the capability from the inside – getting support from the Executive and other data stakeholders to the point where they want you to exist because you are going to make their life easier or less risky. This journey is also going to involve a lot of discussion and education because until you turn up at their door with a copy of the DMBOK under your arm, most individuals won't know anything about data management.

ABOUT THE AUTHOR

Andy Peyton is a long-time veteran of enterprise data management. He started his IT career as a programmer developing software for various branches of the military where he gained an appreciation for the operational cost of software faults and data errors - there's no pushing a reset button at Mach 1.

He gradually moved from front-end systems to back-end enterprise systems and had to address the problems that operational systems suffer when enterprise data doesn't integrate properly or has quality problems. He then moved into consulting roles for various branches of the government, advising on data development, data quality, and data governance policy.

More recently, he has been working as a data architect where he managed major government data migrations and has observed how many of the hard-won lessons of the past aren't being passed on to the data managers of the future.

www.ingramcontent.com/pod-product-compliance
Lightning Source LLC
LaVergne TN
LVHW022108200926
848481LV00003B/1106
9781764718127